SOCIAL MEDIA
MARKETING
for Your
BUSINESS

SOCIAL MEDIA
MARKETING
for Your
BUSINESS

CAROL L. MORGAN, CAPS, CSP, MIRM

 BuilderBooks

Social Media Marketing for Your Business

Elizabeth M.R. Hartke	Acquisitions & Managing Editor
Top Book Designer	Cover Design
María Paula Dufour	Composition
King Printing Co., Inc.	Printing
Gerald M. Howard	NAHB Chief Executive Officer
Lakisha A. Woods CAE	Senior Vice President and Chief Marketing Officer

Disclaimer

Printed in the United States of America

22 21 20 19 18   1 2 3 4 5

ISBN:978-0-86718-764-9
eISBN: 978-0-86718-765-6

Library of Congress CIP information available on request.
For further information, contact

National Association of Home Builders
1201 15th Street NW
Washington, DC 20005
800-223-2665

Visit us online at BuilderBooks.com

CONTENTS

ABOUT THE AUTHOR

Carol L. Morgan, MIRM, CAPS, CSP, has decades of experience as a marketing, public relations and social media expert, strategist, and consultant. She is President of Denim Marketing, a brand she launched in May 2017 that promises to be a comfortable fit for clients. Her original company, Flammer Relations, Inc. will celebrate 19 years in business in 2018. Flammer Relations (dba Denim Marketing) is based in the metro Atlanta area and works nationwide with builders, developers, mortgage companies, construction product manufacturers, apartment developers, banks, and others in the housing and construction industry.

Carol created the nationally-ranked and award-winning real estate blog www. AtlantaRealEstateForum.com in 2006. In fact, she launched several blogs that year, including www.LuxuryRealEstateForum.com, www.GreenBuiltBlog.com and www. FiftyPlusHousing.com. These sites were early pioneers in the blogging space, and because of Carol's early adoption of blogging, she is often fondly referred to as the "Blogging Queen."

In addition to this book, Carol is the author of *Social Media for Home Builders*, *Social Media for Home Builders 2.0*, and *Social Media 3.0*. Carol was on the panel that presented the first social media presentation at the International Builders Show in 2007.

Carol teaches seminars on marketing and social media to companies and associations nationwide. She has spoken at numerous trade shows and conferences, including the NAHB International Builders' Show, 21st Century Building Expo, the Remodeling Show and the Great Lakes Builders Show, just to name a few. Her most quoted and retweeted statement is, "What you say doesn't have to be personal, but it must have personality." She often urges her audiences to consider the question, "When you Google your name, do you like what you see?" After all, online reputation is an important part of branding your company.

Carol holds a BA in business and behavioral science from Oglethorpe University. A member of the Greater Atlanta Home Builders' Association, Carol was honored in 2012 as Council Chair of the Year and in 2008 as Associate of the Year. She is a member of the Georgia Chapter of the Public Relations Society of America and a recipient of PRSA's prestigious George Goodwin Award. She is a past chair of NAHB's Professional Women in Building Council and was honored by this group in 2016 with the prestigious Woman of the Year award.

Other honors include the Oglethorpe University 2008 Spirit of Oglethorpe Award, as well as OBIE, Phoenix, APEX, Hermes, and Communicator awards for blogs and client projects.

Carol is the 2018 NAHB Membership Chair and a member of the Associates Council. She proudly holds the MIRM (Masters in Residential Marketing), CAPS (Certified Aging in Place Specialist) and CSP (Certified Sales Professional) designations from NAHB.

Carol is a member of the National Association of Real Estate Editors, Public Relations Society of America and Greater Atlanta Home Builder's Associations' Sales and Marketing and Professional Women in Building councils.

In her free time, Carol likes to garden, cook, travel, and ride horses. She'd like nothing better than to follow "Diners, Drive-ins and Dives" around from city to city. She competes in the dressage arena on her Trakehner mare, Johanna. She lives with her family at their farm, Thistledown, in Cartersville, Georgia.

PREFACE

Why another social media book? While this is my fourth time to share the secrets of social media for business, I have taken a totally different approach than before. Instead of being a click-by-click, "how to" social media guide, this one starts with big picture marketing and talks about "how" social media fits. Marketing today is all digital, meaning that it is all online. Your marketing program must start with a strong foundation comprised of your website, brand, and content. Once that foundation is established, you can build upon it by sending qualified traffic to your website, using a number of tactics.

After talking through what your social media foundation should look like, I dive into specific sites and give tips for maximizing your engagement and interaction on them. I have completed countless social media audits over the years, and one trend continues to appear. Many times, I can't find any reason why a company is sharing the content they are posting. Chances are they are posting it only because it is the first thing that came to mind when they felt a need to feed the machine.

I hope that after reading this book you can step back, take a breath, and think about what your intention is before you post. If you want your audience to engage, you must create a cohesive content plan with a strategy and goals. Getting results while building your social media presence haphazardly may happen occasionally, but long term you will need a blueprint that starts with that strong foundation.

I became immersed in social media in 2005 (it was called "new media" way back then). Lots of people thought I was crazy. I even was told by someone very close to me that my clients didn't understand or appreciate it and that I was wasting my time. I knew then that I was on to something much bigger than my little blog. I responded, "If I don't' do this, I'll be a 40-year-old dinosaur without an agency." I'm not big into math, but let's just say my gut instinct panned out, and I've continued to find ways to work digital and social media plans into strategies for clients—always with an eye on how each site works best for business.

What I have learned over the last 13 years is invaluable. Because I established my company at the intersection of content and search engine optimization, (i.e., blogging), I can effectively maximize content for clients. And today, blogging is still the biggest differentiator for websites that perform well in the search engines. And results are easier to measure than ever.

With the plethora of social media sites now available, businesses may have a hard time keeping up or even knowing where to start. Success with social media—like any marketing strategy—is not about jumping from one "new shiny thing'" to another. You build a winning strategy by carefully setting goals, creating strategy, and targeting audiences.

This book will help you take a long-term approach to building and maintaining an effective marketing strategy with social media as a main component. Happy reading! Please connect with me online and let me know what questions you have!

Carol@DenimMarketing.com

www.Facebook.com/DenimMarketing

www.Linkedin.com/in/carolmorganflammer

www.Twitter.com/DenimMarketing

www.Pinterest.com/DenimMarketing

www.Instagram.com/DenimMarketing

www.Snapchat.com/DenimMarketing

www.CarolMorgan.net

www.DenimMarketing.com

ACKNOWLEDGMENTS

I dedicate this book to my father, Hugh W. Morgan. Although he is no longer with us, his memory lives on in so many ways. A visionary who built home computers in the late 1970s, Daddy encouraged (really insisted) that I take a computer programming class in 1983. I told him that I would never need to use a computer for anything in my life, but I took the class anyway as it was easier than arguing with him. Daddy really enjoyed walking through my office and saying, "How many computers do you own now, dear?" This was something we laughed about from 1999 to 2016.

A huge thanks to everyone who inspired and supported me while I wrote yet another book! Especially to my best friend, Renita Davis, who kept me on task and provided me with a sounding board for the outline and direction of the book.

A special thanks goes to the entire Denim Marketing team. When confronted with unexpected change, you embraced it and helped build something that is truly a comfortable fit. You are the wind beneath my wings. The Denim team is successful because of each of you and your hard work and dedication. Thank you so much to Courtney Rogers, Mandy Holm, Amanda Meade, Bailey Thompson and Jennifer Luitweiler. I am impressed by your creativity and the level at which you care on a daily basis. An extra thanks to Mandy for providing me with Snapchat expertise—now will you stop snapping pictures of rush hour traffic to me? ;)

I extend a heartfelt thanks to my son, Forrest, who not only believes in me, but is the reason that I started my company 19 years ago. To my mother, sister, and brother, I love each of you very much. I'm glad we have each other's support in good and bad times. An extra, special thanks to my brother, David Morgan, who built my first blogs in 2006—www.AtlantaRealEstateForum.com, www.GreenBuiltBlog.com, www.LuxuryRealEstateForum.com, www.CarolinaRealEstateForum.com and www.FiftyPlusHousing.com. He taught me about SEO, and opened a world of opportunity for me and my clients.

Finally, thanks to all of my clients and friends who embrace social media and the internet and work to become more engaged and more effective every day.

SOCIAL MEDIA
IS EVERYWHERE

1

For years, home builders built homes, and buyers came. That's no longer true in the industry, and it's never been true in social media. It may seem like the messages that appear in your timeline are added with little forethought or preparation, and that's probably true in some cases. However, using social media effectively and consistently to influence buying behavior is as dependent on a strong foundation as is the structural integrity of the homes you're building. Social media is one aspect of much bigger marketing plan, but can't be ignored. Your company needs to be there and it must be managed. Much like a garden, you reap what you sow and it won't weed itself.

If you're wondering why you should bother to invest the resources into a successful social media or digital marketing program, I'll ask you first to take a look at your own life. Be honest…have you or any decision maker in your household ever been influenced by something you saw on social media to buy a product? Try a restaurant? Add a visit to some exotic locale to your bucket list? Vote for a particular candidate?

Okay, we won't get into politics, but research shows that people are making choices based on what they see online. And even if they aren't taking an immediate action, they're being influenced by what they see. The exposure needs to last only a few seconds for them to be influenced. This is also true for all of those billions of people on social media. And it includes people who may someday buy your homes.

Of course, you want to do more than just create an impression on future potential buyers. You want to. . .

Wait. What *do* you want?

We're going to help you figure that out *before* getting into specifics about the different must-haves for your social media and marketing toolbox and the social media sites themselves. Don't skip the important step of determining your goals! If you know what you hope to accomplish, you'll read the remainder of the book with a better understanding of which sites and which tools will help you get there.

WHO IS USING THE INTERNET AND HOW ARE THEY ACCESSING IT?

Internet usage has grown considerably since 2000. Nearly nine out of every 10 Americans are now online. Pew Research Center[1] has identified four interesting key trends:

1 · 77 percent of Americans now own a smart phone. The biggest increases are attributed to lower income Americans and those over 50 years old.

2 · Nearly three-quarters (73 percent) of Americans now have broadband service at home.

3 · Almost seven-in-ten (69 percent) Americans utilize social media. The use of social media sites is very popular with young adults, as 86 percent of 18- to 29-year-olds are social media users. However, don't discount older Americans. The majority of those ages 30–49 (80 percent) and 50–64 (64 percent) use social media as well. Only about one-third (34 percent) of Americans 65 and older currently use social media. And this figure continues to grow.

4 · 51 percent of Americans now own a tablet. Usage of tablets continues to grow.

Other statistics from Pew Research Center[2] show that nearly eight-in-ten online Americans (79 percent) now use Facebook, more than *double* the share that uses Twitter (24 percent), Pinterest (31 percent), Instagram (32 percent) or LinkedIn (29 percent). On a total population basis (accounting for Americans who do not use the internet at all), that means that 68 percent of all U.S. adults are Facebook users, while 28 percent use Instagram, 26 percent use Pinterest, 25 percent use LinkedIn and 21 percent use Twitter.

WHO USES EACH SOCIAL MEDIA PLATFORM?

Usage of the major social media platforms varies by factors such as age, gender and educational attainment. Pew Research Center[3] has broken down who is using each social media platform. For example, 69 percent of women use Facebook, and 67 percent of men. By reviewing the ages of the people using Facebook it is easy to see that if you are targeting U.S. consumers ages 18–64, this is the biggest platform by a landslide. Facebook also boasts the best educated users of all the social platforms with 77 percent of college graduates using the platform. The research also includes an income level breakdown and details whether users are urban, suburban, or rural.

HOW NEW HOME BUYERS USE SOCIAL MEDIA

First, let's talk about how homebuyers actually use social media in their decision making process. A 2017 ViaSearch[4] survey reveals that 72 percent of home buyers think it is important for home builders to use social media (fig. 1.1). Of the sites they use, Facebook was cited as very to extremely useful by 50 percent of buyers. Surprisingly, Google+ was second with 45 percent of buyers saying it is very to extremely useful (fig. 1.2). While this might seem strange, think about it: when you search a company on Google from your PC, the company's Google Business page shows up in the right side bar with their map information and reviews and this is tied into Google+. YouTube took the third spot in the survey with 23 percent of buyers reporting that it is very to extremely useful. Houzz, LinkedIn, Instagram and Pinterest each received 10 percent to tie for fourth place. Twitter and SnapChat were each seven percent.

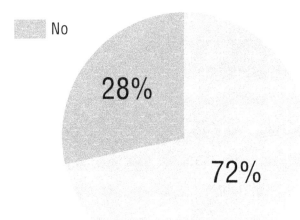

No

28%

72%

Yes

Figure 1.1 | Is it important for builders to have a social media presence?

Source: Reprinted with permission from 2017 ViaSearch New Home Buyer Report.

50%

45%

23%

10%   10%   10%   10%

7%   7%

Facebook   Google+   YouTube   Houzz   LinkedIn   Instagram   Pinterest   Twitter   Snapchat

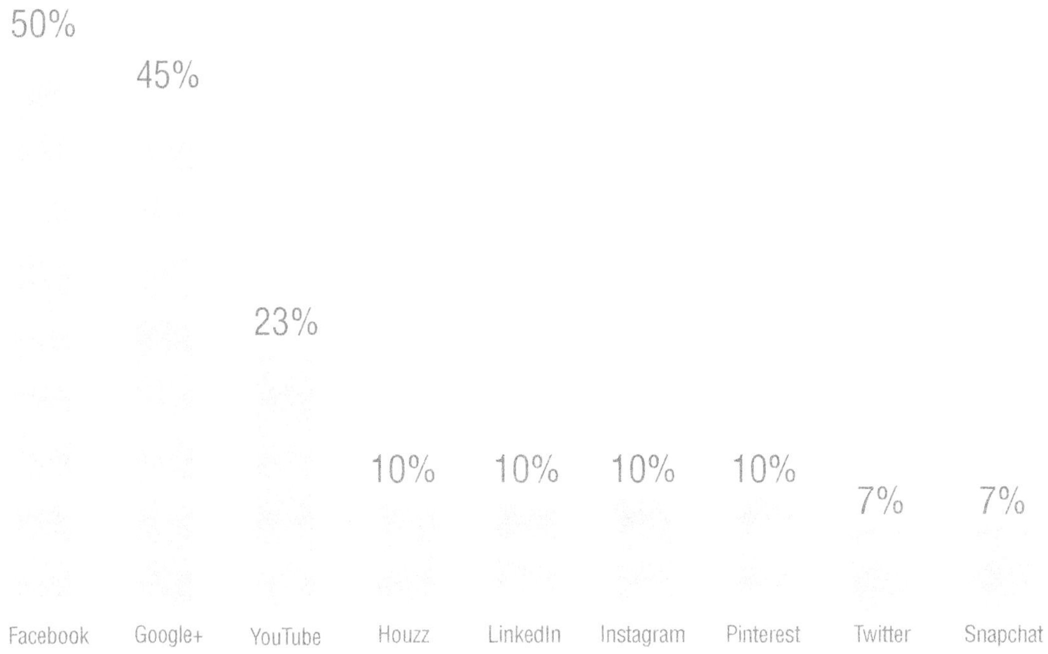

Figure 1.2 | What did you want to see in new home ads?

Source: Reprinted with permission from 2017 ViaSearch New Home Buyer Report.

There are several other trends from the ViaSearch survey that are important to note. New home buyers indicate that when they are looking at homes the availability of informational videos, virtual reality and 3D tours are very important. Seventy five to 80 percent indicated that these interactive visuals are very important to extremely important in the home shopping process (fig. 1.3).

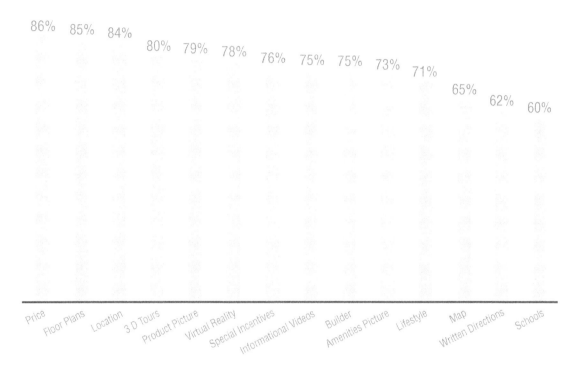

Figure 1.3 | What did you want to see in new home ads?

Source: Reprinted with permission from 2017 ViaSearch New Home Buyer Report.

Equally important to note is the importance of consumer review sites. Buyers rank these in order of importance: Google+, Facebook, Yelp, the Yellow Pages, and Angie's List (fig. 1.4). Buyers are using these online review sites to determine how companies respond to warranty issues and other customer complaints. After all, the response and care that one customer receives will not be dissimilar to the care and response they receive if or when they have a problem. Acting now to establish a proactive program to get reviews from happy customers is important. (This is discussed more in-depth in Chapter 4 Reputation Management.)

Figure 1.4 | Which consumer review sites did you use?

Source: Reprinted with permission from 2017 ViaSearch New Home Buyer Report.

THE
BIG PICTURE

2

Before we dive into integrated marketing strategy and what that looks like, let's take a step back and look at the BIG picture. Today's consumers are savvier than ever. We've been through a recession and the "field of dreams" is in the distant past. There is no guarantee that if you build it, they will come. In fact, one thing that is certain is that the 4Ps—price, product, promotion and place must be in alignment. If your product is in the wrong school system, or overpriced or missing key elements, there is no guarantee that any amount of marketing will overcome this discrepancy. Today's market is unforgiving. And when it comes to new home communities, the biggest competitor isn't that new home neighborhood down the street; it is all the resale homes. After all, resales account for 80–90 percent of all transactions, depending on the market. And according to John Hunt, market analyst, principal and founder of MarketNsight, "New homes must be priced within 10 to 20 percent of comparable resale homes to sell with any velocity." He calls this the 80/20 rule of homebuilding. So, of the 4Ps, it is crucial to have price, product and place correct, because no amount of promotion will make up for one or more of these being out of sync.

What constitutes a successful integrated marketing strategy? In many ways, this is easier today than ever. The shift to online makes it simple to see what works and what doesn't and to measure return on investment (ROI). A successful business needs to create a strong digital foundation for marketing that centers on their website (and news or blog), branding, and content (and search engine optimization). Focus on these main assets to form a strong nucleus that all other tactics can enhance and refer customers to.

This approach to marketing creates an effective and flexible marketing program that includes any tactic you can think of from content development and syndication, search engine optimization (SEO), social media, public relations, creative, reputation management, email marketing, and media/advertising management. Each tactic is utilized to drive traffic to your core assets. This focus builds an interconnected strategy that drives traffic to the website and proves ROI. Interactive elements are intertwined with traditional media for a more effective reach. This increases website traffic and referrals, as well as conversations and engagement. The goal for social media within this strategy is to create a framework for interactions and engagement such that your raving fans start to post applicable positive content to your social media pages.

YOUR WEBSITE

Websites must be trendy. By this I mean that they must have a current design, include video or 3D tours or virtual reality and be responsive. If the design of your website looks like it was done at the dawn of the World Wide Web, it is time to update it. Consumers want to work with and buy from companies that are up-to-date. After all, if your website is archaic, are your building standards dated too?

Video and interactivity is so important. Consumers like to thoroughly research all plans before they walk into your sales center, and the best way to do this is via video or 3D or virtual reality. This is a trend that is going to continue to increase. Presently, 75–80 percent of buyers expect to be able to see these types of tours. With Generation Next— today's teens who use Snapchat and Instagram to communicate—we expect this trend to continue.

Responsive websites will return a result that makes sense whether they are being viewed on a PC, tablet, or smartphone. With approximately 50 percent of all searches starting on a smartphone, this isn't an audience to be ignored. There is nothing worse than wanting information and finding a result that can't be viewed from a phone.

In addition to being trendy, your website must also be a lead capturing machine. This means that whether traffic gets to your site from Google pay-per-click (search marketing), through organic search, or through referral traffic, the traffic should stick. The consumer should be able to find what they are looking for within a few clicks and ultimately make it to the Contact Us form and complete it. Being a lead capture machine also means that each page of the website needs to have a Call to Action (CTA), whether that is a contact form, a phone call, or another action such as downloading driving directions or a floorplan.

BRANDING

A company's brand is the next key to a strong digital foundation. Brand is supported by social media, reputation management, public relations, email marketing, advertising campaigns, blogging, video, 3D, etc.

Create a brand that resonates with buyers and is easily recognizable from site to site online, in print, and in person. It should be easy to identify on the company website, Facebook page, and Yelp. Utilize colors and fonts that your target audience can relate to, and make sure your brand promise or USP (unique selling proposition) is something that can be conveyed easily in person, over the phone, and in print.

Take a few minutes to review your corporate brand across all sites and all digital assets as well as print. Make sure that your company's logo on your website matches across all other sites where it appears. Work with a graphic designer to ensure that your logo is sized/shaped appropriately for each site. Once you have confirmed that your visual brand is consistent, take a few minutes to ask your employees to give you their elevator speech and listen as they answer the phone.

CONTENT

Content is the final area to focus on to ensure that you have built a strong digital foundation. One that is both critical-and often overlooked. Content plays an important role on your website not only for browsers and buyers, but also for the search engines. Having content that clearly explains the company's products, services, areas served and differentiations will give the search engines something to index. Websites also need to be built with proper SEO. Yes, title tags and metadata matter, and so does the content on each page.

Since Google's release of the Panda and Penguin algorithms, original quality content is more important than ever. All websites have content and some level of traffic. To get more traffic than your competition, include a well-built, optimized blog or news section and add fresh, original, quality content on an ongoing basis. This content should directly relate back to the 4Ps and be truly unique. If you could post your content on a competitor's site and no one would know the difference, you are missing the mark. We will talk more about blogging in Chapter 15 Other Digital Marketing. There are certainly other tactics that you should take advantage of for a strong search engine optimization program, but content is the cornerstone of SEO.

Once you have a strong digital foundation for marketing that centers on your website, branding, and content, it will be easy to build a network of tactics and sites around it to refer back to it. It is important to build the marketing strategy within this integrated network and not as silos. For those who have followed me for awhile, you know that I think silos are for cows. A successful marketing program will include tactics that work in tandem, not create a silo.

CONTENT PLANNING

A comprehensive content strategy is easier to create than you may think. Take a few minutes and think about everything going on in your business. Now get out a piece of paper and a pen and write everything down. Once you have listed all of the new products, community news, completion dates for projects, industry events that you sponsor or participate in, promotions, grand openings, company news and other milestones—like company anniversaries—then start scheduling the stories you have to share each month. By writing everything down and placing the content on the month you plan to run it, you will start to develop a calendar. Depending on how much you have to share, your calendar might cover just one quarter, or you might have enough information to flow across an entire year.

Create a plan for content on your website, blog, and social media sites. All of these sites perform better with fresh content for consumers to read and the search engines to find. When you think of content, remember that it isn't just written words. Vary your content between photos, videos, infographics, articles, graphics, etc.

In addition to a content strategy, a well-planned social media strategy also incorporates a plan for:

- Who is making the posts

- How often posts are made

- A plan for gaining followers and interacting with them

- Reputation management and customer service

- Setting and measuring goals

Who will post?

Decide upfront who is responsible to posting content to each site. If you have an in-house marketing team, most likely they will be responsible for ensuring posts are made either by an internal team or an agency. There is no perfect answer to who should run the social media sites, but the person should be organized, well-spoken, and want to engage with others in conversation. Some companies choose to put a team together to keep the sites active—perhaps this team is a combination of people with different talents. One person may write all the blogs, while another syndicates them to all of the social media sites taking into consideration all of the nuances of each individual site. With an organized plan you can easily have multiple people involved in posting. If you are a small company or even a large company with an over-tasked marketing team, you should consider outsourcing the content and posting to an agency in order to keep your team on task. (See Chapter 16 Managing Your Social Media Program on in-house versus using an agency.)

Frequency of Use

Define how often posts should be made—the more frequently, the better. Try to update your social media sites daily, or at least every few days. Of course, this is optimal. You might not have the staff or the content to post this often. Determining how often to post is definitely influenced by number of staff, the number of social media sites and the amount of content.

For a small company, we'd recommend two to three blog posts a month, Facebook posts two to three days a week, and then it depends on what other sites you have and what is important to you. For instance, every time you post a new blog, it can be posted to Facebook, Google+ and LinkedIn.

ny should write six to eight blogs posts a month, post to Facebook
Twitter several times a day, repurpose all blog content across multiple
stagram at least once a week, and make sure to incorporate Google+,
dln, and YouTube. (See Chapter 5 for more information on the importance of video.)

Followers and Interactions

How will the pages attract new followers? Where will the pages be promoted? Will they be cross promoted from email signatures, in email marketing, on advertisements, on the website, etc.? Will the social media team help to find followers? Or, will advertising be used to find and attract followers? Make sure that your content isn't a deal breaker once they get to the page. Content needs to be fun in order for consumers to believe it is worth following. Just posting updates isn't enough; you need interaction from your followers (shares, likes, etc.), so post content that they want to read and share. Don't make the mistake of sharing other people's content. Despite what others may tell you about content, consumers follow you to learn about your company, not to read watered down content that could be running on any site that is similar to yours.

Encourage interactions with your followers—you can even reward them. Give out gift cards randomly to people who comment on your posts. Ask them to post content to your page. Find ways to get followers to interact, engage, and even post for you!

Customer Service

Strong customer service can go a long way in strengthening your business' brand and improving customer relationships, and social media has become an outlet to do just that. It's important for businesses and brands to think of social media as a huge customer service opportunity.

Consumers have figured out that a great place to air their complaints about a business is on social media or through online review sites. Customers like to complain on social media because it is a public forum and their issues are more likely to be addressed. Also, if they are really mad at a company, it is the perfect way to share their grievances with other people and influence whether that person might make a purchase from the company in the future...or not.

OPEN HOUSE
GUEST SIGN-IN CARD

Name _____

Email Address: _____

Phone Cell / Home _____

Bedrooms: _____ Baths: _____

Pool: Y N Price Range _____

Waterfront: Y N Dock: _____

Do you currently have a home to sell? Y N

Are you currently working with another Realtor Y N

Social Media Today[1] shares some interesting statistics on how customers use social media to solve customer service issues are very interesting.

- One-third of social media users prefer to contact companies via social media. It is preferred over phone or email

- Estimates show as many as 67 percent of consumers using social networks like to use Twitter and Facebook to seek resolution for issues

- Customers will spend 20–40 percent more with companies that engage with customers via social media

- Nearly 70 percent of consumers have said that they have used social media for issues to do with customer service on at least one occasion

To build an online customer service program, first find out which social media sites your customers prefer. It's hard to go wrong with Facebook and Twitter, but there may be discussions about your business on other social media sites as well. Look for conversations about your company, respond to comments, and answer questions.

The key to great customer service on social media is a fast response time. Reply to customer complaints or concerns as quickly as possible. Generally, aim to respond within three minutes (faster if possible). Many big builders and big brands employ an online concierge, internet marketing coordinator, marketing assistant or a social media manager and this position is tasked with monitoring social media and answering customer inquiries and complaints as quickly possible.

Facebook pages now show how quickly companies respond to the messages they receive. This displays on the right sidebar in the 'About' section. While "typically responds instantly" is a great ranking to have, "typically responds in a few hours" is a bit less desirable. The faster and more consistently a business responds to customer questions and complaints sent through Messages, the more positive it will reflect on the page. In fact, Facebook even gives customers a badge for excellent response time. The "very responsive to messages badge" is earned by Pages that respond super quickly to private messages. To get the badge, a Page must achieve a response rate of 90 percent and a response time of 15 minutes or less over the course of seven days.

Facebook also has a reviews section, although many businesses opt to hide this section. The reviews range from one to five stars and offer the opportunity to comment as well. Customers like to use this feature to complain, so it is important to encourage happy customers to use it as well.

On Twitter, the key to customer service is speed. Reply as quickly as possible to their direct message or tweet. You can follow them, reply to them, or even direct message them to keep the conversation private.

Acknowledge customer's posts, regardless of what site they are on. Being ignored or deleted typically makes them even madder. It is best to acknowledge them with a personal response. People like to know who they're talking to, so give your name when you respond to help create a connection. Your response could be as simple as, "This is Carol Morgan with XYZ Corporation and we are so sorry you have experienced a problem. Please call me direct at xxx-xxx-xxxx so that we can help you with this situation."

Be friendly and helpful in your communication with customers, even when they are being ridiculous or difficult. Show genuine concern and make an effort to help them through their problems. It's all about helping someone, which in turn helps win over other customers and strengthen your business. Since social media is a public forum, remember that what you post will be seen by many people, not just the one you are answering.

The goal of social media is to build relationships. Providing excellent customer service shows the company cares about its customers and keeping them happy. Build relationships with customers and turn them into raving fans. If you get lucky, these raving fans will become brand advocates and jump in and answer customer service questions for you.

GOAL
SETTING 3

When it comes to your digital marketing program, begin with the end in mind. If you don't know where you are going, you won't get there. There are a lot of different goals and objectives that you can have for your social media tactics. By defining specific, measurable goals related to social media efforts, you will discover what works and what doesn't. Do you want more onsite traffic? Do you want more website traffic? Is your Facebook engagement low, but your follower count high? Think through what you want to achieve follow this process:

- Set measurable goals

- Determine a specific timeframe

- Choose your implementation team

- Determine how goals will be measured (tracking website clicks, completed contact forms, clicks for directions, increased followers, increased engagement, etc.)

Your business could have a variety of goals for social media. And, each action you take on social media should have a goal. Don't just post without some sort of intent. Determine what action you want your audience to take and then post in a way that encourages the desired result. Here are six goals you should consider when building your social media program:

    1 · Increased website traffic

2 · Improved website search engine optimization

3 · Reputation management

4 · Engage with followers (customers, advocates, potential customers)

5 · Increased brand awareness

6 · Completed website contact forms

INCREASED WEBSITE TRAFFIC

Utilizing social media effectively can help you increase the traffic to your website. Use social media to send traffic to your website. There are a couple of easy ways to do this. First, syndicate your blog posts to various social media sites. Make sure that when a follower clicks on a post, to read more that they get taken to the full article on your blog. Another way to increase website traffic is to make sure that every single post, regardless of what site it is on, links to a relevant page on your company's website.

More traffic equals more buyers, so don't miss this easy opportunity to drive traffic to the website. Post relevant content on blogs, social networking sites, and online public relations, incorporating links to the website. This will also increase the number of referring URLs for your website. Links provide potential buyers more opportunities to click and connect to your website and find your business online. Think of it as weaving a bigger web or placing a sign spinner on just the right corner to send traffic exactly where you want it.

Appearing in all the places where consumers are already online (like the social net-working sites) helps to create a bigger funnel of potential buyers: You capture many users' attention and then focus their search so they eventually land on your website. Leading more traffic to your website can increase the number of lead conversions because effective social media programs tend to garner more qualified leads. This is because they are already a warm lead. If a potential buyer is on one of your social media sites, chances are they have already decided that you are among the top two or three companies they are considering.

Organic Content versus Paid

Social media is an established marketing staple. Embraced by large and small companies because of the volume of users on all the sites, social media has the power to reach hundreds, even thousands, with targeted messages. Facebook alone has two billion active users (a quarter of the population of the planet). So, obviously it makes sense to have a presence on these sites and to be engaged with buyers. But with all of the various algorithms, knowing how to reach your target audience and knowing how to get the best return on investment can be confusing.

As the owner of a marketing agency, I get asked this question a lot, "Should I pay for ads on social media or just rely on organic posts?" Well, the answer is "You should do both."

So, what should a company post on social media—organic or paid content? It is definitely a blend of both. Social media is about conversations and great content. To get interactions on social media, you need a combination of posts that pull followers into your page, and then you can post content that pushes out to them. Let me explain: All social media sites have algorithms that determine what people on the site see. Just because someone follows your page, it does not ensure that they see any of your posts. In order to see your posts on Facebook, followers actually have to be engaged with your page. This means that they must like, share, or comment on posts.

The challenge is to create content that followers want to engage with. One way to do this is through a combination of paid and organic posts. For instance, you could run a social media promotion to highlight a model home opening. To enter, a follower would need to post a photo of themselves at the model home on Facebook with the hashtag #BuilderModelOpeningContest. A winner could be picked at random from all the entries over a two-week period. The winner might get a prize such as $100 gift card to Pottery Barn or Home Depot. To magnify the reach of the contest, the home builder could run Facebook ads to promote the contest page or post. By running ads on Facebook that target followers, as well as the builder's main demographic, the reach of the contest is both extended and magnified. Now everyone who has liked, shared, or commented on the contest will see more of the page's information on a daily basis. By hosting the contest and advertising it, you have effectively pulled followers into your page. Now, the next time you post about a new home plan or new agent, more people will see it.

Organic reach of Facebook posts is typically only 2 to 20 percent of a page's followers, so it is important to enhance reach with paid ads. The variety of paid options on this site ranges from website clicks, to page likes, event promotions, sponsored posts, and much more. Using a variety of paid posts and organic posts provides better reach. Your budget does not have to be huge to be effective. It could be as little as $250 a month or as much as $5,000 a month. It depends on your goals.

Improved SEO

Search engine optimization uses specific strategies to boost a website's ranking in search results for a variety of keywords or phrases. Both on-page (on the website) and off-page (e.g., links, articles, other sites) can achieve positive organic results. Organic results appear because of their relevance to the term being searched. They are not paid advertisements or pay-per-click results. The term "search engine marketing" typically refers to marketing via both paid search. If you are purchasing this service, ask what you are actually buying. Often companies selling a search engine marketing service will call it search engine optimization.

One way to improve organic search results and the relevance of a site is to create quality links from quality sites to your website. And, yes, I know you have heard terrible things about link farms and link building. But, not all links are bad. Think of these links as third-party credibility, much like what you get when the local newspaper runs a story about you. So, always link from the various social media sites back to your website. This will not only improve the quantity of your website traffic, but the traffic should be quality traffic. And best of all: it will improve your SEO.

REPUTATION MANAGEMENT

After managing a number of highly visible reputation management campaigns over the past decade, I'm compelled to say that it is imperative to have a process for handling customer concerns and complaints, as well as warranty issues. Deleting that unhappy buyer's comments from your Facebook page will likely only escalate the problem. Implement a plan for customer service and consider including customer surveys and a loyalty program as part of it.

Your reputation is critical. Your customers start their search for your product or service online. Make sure you can answer these questions with a positive response: When you Google your name, do you like what you see? More importantly, when your pro-spective buyers Google your name, do **they** like what they see?

If you don't like your search engine results page (SERP), you should implement a reputation management program right away! If you find an unhappy customer's posts or reviews on page one of your company's results, you can be certain that potential customers will find them too. To manage your reputation, fill your page-one SERPs with desirable results. A well-built blog and a website with proper SEO should appear consistently among the first four results for your name. You can easily fill up the rest of your page-one results with posts to online PR and social networking sites such as Facebook, Pinterest, Trulia®, Twitter, YouTube, and Flickr®—to name just a few favor-ites. We go into much more detail in Chapter 4 Reputation Management.

ENGAGE WITH FOLLOWERS

It is possible to have several thousands of followers on Facebook, Twitter, or Pinterest, but not have any engagement with them. The algorithms used by the various social networking sites ensure that followers see the content they are most interested in. And, this means that if they have not interacted with your brand recently, they are not seeing your posts. To resolve this, create a mix of messages to push out to your fol-lowers and messages that pull followers back to you.

For instance, hosting a contest on your Pinterest page to "decorate your dream model home" pulls followers to your page. This is especially true if the contest is promoted on all of your other social media sites and has a small Facebook advertising spend with it, as well as a great prize. By pulling these followers into Pinterest and Facebook, when you post the finished model home photos and push this content live, they are more likely to see them and like the album.

Customers and potential customers want to discover your company's personality and culture. By engaging in conversations, interacting with others, and forming relation-ships, you are giving them the opportunity to get to know you.

Consumers who embrace social media want to know what's in it for them. (They are asking, "What's in it for me?") The main reason consumers friend, fan, or follow brands is to get something. It's all about the "me" in social media. As a business, you must provide social networkers with a reason to follow you, such as a coupon or incentive just for the fans that Follow you on Facebook, or information that educates them or helps them solve a problem. And, I can't stress enough that they want *your* company's information, not generic content that could be posted anywhere.

To some extent, you must create your audience by starting with the groups that already have buy-in to your company. There are four groups of people that will engage with you and talk about you if you approach them in the right order:

1 · **Your internal team.** Your staff are the most likely people to support your social media channels from the start. They already believe in the company and believe in its messages, so ask them to like, comment and share them. Consider hosting an internal contest, as well as give them some training.

2 · **Influencers.** These are your raving fans and cheerleaders, your industry partners including mortgage bankers, Realtors, trade partners and all of those industry friends you network with. They already know you and chances are, if you interact with them a little on social media, they will reciprocate and interact with you.

3 · **Happy customers.** They have already picked you and are likely to share their experience with others if you ask. Develop a strategy for getting them involved in your social media program. Consider hosting mini contests. For instance, for fall you could ask your happy homeowners to post photos of themselves with their homes decorated for fall. Then give a prize randomly from participants or choose the best décor and reward it.

4 · **Prospects.** This is perhaps the hardest group to get to interact. They are most likely to consume content on your page, but not engage. They want to see what specials or promotions you are offering and how you interact with current customers. Once you have the first three groups on this list interacting, it is much easier to get prospects to join in.

It's not just about social media though; the same principles apply in all facets of your brand advocacy and your marketing strategy. Use the power of your employees to start spreading your brand's message; in other words, turn them into brand ambassadors.

INCREASE BRAND AWARENESS

Your social networking should fulfill your brand promise and positioning. If you promote that you are a customer-service-oriented company, your customers might just test you on social media. Companies large and small, including competitors that you may or may not be aware of, are building their brand online every minute. Online branding is a comparatively inexpensive versus using traditional media. A first step in branding your company online is ensuring that your company logo and colors are on every website and social site that you participate in. Not only should they be there, but they should be the same on each site. This is your chance to extend your brand beyond your own website and printed materials. You will avoid confusing consumers if you have a clear brand and messaging. Brand goes beyond your logo and promises made in a print ad: it is a lasting impression of your company that can begin with how the phones are answered, how you sign your email messages, and what internet users find when they search your name online.

Online consumers also learn about you by where they don't find you. When they Google your name, can prospects find you? Do you appear at the top of SERP results when they Google your unique selling proposition (USP)? (Yes, USPs apply to online as well as traditional marketing.) Do they find you or your main competitor first? Prospective buyers must be able to locate you where they think you should be, not only in the search engines, but also on social media sites. Can they find and engage with you on Facebook, Instagram, Pinterest and your blog? This is key, look back at the ViaSearch results on where buyers think you need to be if you wonder why it is important.

COMPLETED WEBSITE CONTACT FORMS

We all want more leads. Right? And more sales. By using social media advertising to send clicks to the company's website contact form you can increase the number of forms generated each month. Landing pages with get contact information from them. Social media helps to create a sales funnel; you can use social lead capture can be created for various social media sites or campaigns. Because these browsers or followers already have a warm introduction to the company, it is easier to media to interact with customers and prospective clients in order to convert them from leads to prospects and ultimately, to buyers.

REPUTATION
MANAGEMENT 4

M anaging your online reputation has become a critical part of marketing. First, you need to know what other people are saying. Start by researching what is online about your company. Google your company name. Search the hard terms, like your company name plus "sucks" and "reviews" and other terms that you can think of that might be out there. Learn what is being said by making use of listening and monitoring tools, like Google Alerts, Twitter searches, Sprout Social and Hoot Suite, to track the online conversations about your business.

When you Google your company name, the first page of search results is the most important. In our reputation management programs, we work to fill up the first page with authentic, helpful and useful information about a business including a business' website, Google Business Page, Google+, Facebook, LinkedIn, YouTube, Twitter and news about your company from trustworthy news sites. Proactively publishing positive news and using social media fills up your page one results with what you want prospective customers to see.

A corporate blog acts as a syndication hub; you can publish all of your business news there, improve search results and increase traffic. Posting news to public relations sites is another way to help reach those goals; some of these sites are free, some are paid, and posting can easily be done by your public relations or marketing agency.

We see several different reputation management problems, and while they all require effort to fix them, some are far worse than others. Here is the nitty gritty of the various issues:

- **Bad search engine result pages.** I often ask, "When you Google your name, do you like what you see?" In a perfect world, a company's page one results should all be positive and about them (versus about some other company that happens to share the same name). When you Google your name and find sites like Ripoff Report, Pissed Consumer, Better Business Bureau, Yelp, Google and Glassdoor with negative reviews on page one, this is bad. In some instances you can respond to and mitigate these bad reviews, but in the worst cases a full blown reputation management campaign will need to be launched to push these results to page two and beyond.

- **One or two bad reviews.** Maybe your SERPs look just fine, but when you Google your name with the word Reviews after it, you find a bad review on Google or Yelp. These reviews should be responded to on the site where they appear. Every effort should be made to turn the negative into a positive. Ideally, the person whoposted the negative review will come back and respond that the problem has been resolved.

- **No reviews at all.**This is certainly not as disconcerting as bad search engine results or bad reviews, but it is important to have a plan to get positive reviews. After all, potential customers are going to research companies online before they buy from them.

MAKE THE MOST OF GOOGLE

Setting up your company's Google presence is important, as this ensures that your business information shows up on Google Maps, in Search, and in other places on Google. Google reviews show up on your Google My Business page, as well as reviews from other places on the web. To add your business information use Google My Business. You can simply "Google it" to find it. Make sure that you create a local Google My Business listing. Google+ Pages do not show up on Maps or Search. Also, Google My Business listings will only work with locations that have a physical storefront or that serve customers at the location.

CUSTOMERS SEARCH FOR INFORMATION... AND REASSURANCE

New customers want to feel secure with the decision they have made to buy from a company. Looking at customer reviews helps establish credibility from a third party, and this gives new customers a sense of security. According to statistics compiled by Invesp[1], 90 percent of consumers read online reviews before visiting a business, and 88 percent of consumers trust online reviews as much as personal recommendations. Positive reviews are powerful tools for converting browsers into buyers.

BrightLocal's Local Consumer Review Survey[2] found that 40 percent of consumers form an opinion by reading just one, two, or three reviews and 68 percent say positive reviews make them trust a local business more.

What exactly does a person look for in a testimonial or a review?

- **Credibility.** Is the company trustworthy and credible? Can I establish this from a third party? Do they seem sincere?

- **Similar situation.** Is the person giving the review or testimonial in a similar situation as mine? If I am a first time buyer, I might not be able to relate to the boomer buyer purchasing a move down home especially if it is their third home purchase.

- **Timely.** Is the review recent? If not, how old is it? If it is several years old, how do I know that the company has the same operations team? Generally consumers are going to look for reviews that were made in the last year.

Review sites, like Google+, the YellowPages, SuperPages, Yelp, Angie's List and Facebook, all can help attract customers. So, what is the best way to get reviews? Put very simply, ask for them!

- **Point of purchase display.** Print a small counter-top sign asking for reviews in your lobby, or on a sales center or model home desk.

- **Open house.** At the next agent open house, bring a tablet or iPad and ask the agents in attendance to login to Facebook or Google+ (or site of your preference) and write a review. Perhaps you can even give them a $10 Starbucks gift card as a token of thanks.

- **Business cards or palm cards.** Print business or palm cards and give them to customers, agents, vendors and others that you have a relations hip with. Include information on the card of where to go to write a review. Give these cards to happy customers at the appropriate time—completion of their remodel, closing, final walk through, etc.

- **Email.** Try emailing your best customers with a link to your preferred review site. You could send it to vendors and partners as well.

TESTIMONIALS AND REVIEWS

Testimonials and reviews are very similar, but consumers might think of them as being slightly different. Reviews are customer opinions that are given on third party sites like Yelp or Facebook or Google. A testimonial is any endorsement of a product or service and it could be on your company website or blog as an article or letter, video, graphic, photos, or even a podcast. Both help with the sales process and are great tools to have in the marketing mix.

Get testimonials from happy customers, as soon as possible, at the point of sale, or within a few days following the sale. Help customers put into words the nice things that they have said about the buying process, reminding them of unique selling propositions, like customer service, personalization options, value, etc. You could even offer to draft the testimonial for them and send it to them for their approval, once they have given approval, post it to your website or blog and then to your social media accounts. Perhaps they will even send you a photo of themselves in front of their home to use with the testimonial. These testimonials can be written or in video form. Be sure to get permission to use the customer's testimonial, their name and the community in which they live. And keep in mind that some customers are sensitive to having reviews posted due to privacy concerns.

Turn testimonials into attractive handouts/sales flyers, then post this content on your website, or shared in emails or mailers. Video testimonials are great for posting online and/or linking to in social media posts, e-newsletters and more.

When Online Reviews Go Bad

People trust recommendations from people they know over anything else. And, recent research by Nielsen Social[3] shows that consumer opinions posted online have the biggest influence on purchasing decisions next to recommendations from family and friends. This means that online customer reviews are now more important than TV ads, print ads, corporate websites, radio, etc. Because of the influence that online reviews have on purchasing decisions, businesses are under huge pressure to present positive reviews to boost sales. Unfortunately this causes some companies to make up fake reviews. It has been estimated that as many as one in seven online reviews may be fraudulent.

Review sites, such as Yelp, look for clues that reviews might be fake. And, they will take down reviews that seem phony or were obviously posted by business owners, SEO companies, or reputation management companies. If a lot of reviews are loaded at the same time, they might think those are fake too and remove some of them. This often happens if you ask multiple people to review your company on the same day.

It should go without saying that one way to protect your reputation is by maintaining authentic reviews. An occasional negative review is inevitable, and being deceitful or counterfeit will only damage your brand.

Dealing with Negative Feedback

Negative feedback can be painful for a business, but it can expose real business process problems that need to be addressed. Often, negative reviewers are angry, because they felt that they have been wronged. Sometimes their anger is legitimate, and sometimes it is not. There are also trolls and spammers with no valid reason for being angry with your business, and may be using negative reviews (whether true or not) to promote a competitor's business.

There are several third party rating programs that are used by companies to survey customers and improve business processes. By utilizing these tools, companies can greatly improve their processes and also improve customer service for future customers. Both Guild Quality and Avid Ratings are frequently used by home builders, remodelers, contractors and others in the industry to survey customers.

Responding to Negative Reviews

Don't panic when you receive a negative review. It is inevitable! At some point you will have an unhappy client, so don't panic or hit the delete button. Take a deep breath, and take a little time to think about the complaint and the best way to handle it. Of course, depending on the site, your response might be expected within minutes or hours... not days. Since the review is posted publicly, it is best to respond publicly. Be transparent, positive, sincere, and stay professional. If you need to respond quickly, thank the customer for their feedback, tell them you are sorry that they had an issue and let them know that you are looking into the problem. You might want to simply respond, "I'm so sorry that you have had this experience. Please reach out to me directly at ###-###-### so that I can address your concerns personally."

If research is necessary to determine and resolve the issue, do as much research as possible and then follow up with the customer, providing them with options for a solution. Responding publicly shows other potential buyers that you are taking responsibility for the situation.

Negative reviews can truly damage a business, and there are instances where businesses have taken legal action. Statements of opinion are generally legally protected, so the legal avenues for addressing defamatory comments can be tricky. Most review sites are protected from liability for the content posted by their users. Because of this, these publishers have little incentive to take down content without a court order. And, unfortunately, most of these sites seem to rank very well in the search engines.

When defamatory comments are posted, you should first attempt to resolve the issue with the person that posted it. Next, determine if the comment violates the site's terms of service in any way. If it does, the site may remove the statement for you. If you can't resolve the issue directly with the person or the site, then you may want to seek legal counsel to obtain a court order for the site to remove the statements.

The bottom line is that you need to be proactive in obtaining positive reviews and testimonials from your happy customers.

MOBILE, VISUALS, AND HASHTAGS: 5
SOCIAL MEDIA
MUST-HAVES

Getting noticed on social media isn't easy, but there are some things you can do to break through the clutter, help your posts get seen, and even attract followers. Think mobile, and make sure that all of your social media sites look good on mobile. This includes header images, logos, ads and posts. Just because it looks good on your desk top, does not mean it will look good on mobile. Visuals attract attention. Make sure your photos, graphics and videos are fun and catchy so that people will respond to them. Finally, using hashtags effectively can help attract more followers with similar interest.

MOBILE

Ninety five percent of Americans own a cell phone. And of those, 77 percent own a smartphone. This has increased from just 35 percent in the first survey of smartphone ownership conducted by Pew Research Center[1] in 2011.

For businesses, this means that it is super important to make sure your website is mobile, and that your social media presence is completely optimized for smartphones and tablets. And, let's be clear, just because they can open your website from their smartphone that does *not* mean that it is mobile. If a potential buyer has to pinch and zoom, the site isn't mobile. And, if it is built so poorly, then a shopper can't find what they expect to. They need to be able to find directions, a phone number, hours of operation, and much more within several clicks. Consumers demand immediate response and instant gratification. Does your mobile strategy accomplish this? Does your mobile experience create a specific experience for each customer? Can they find answers to their questions? And, can they find them quickly? Or, do they get frustrated with a slow page load time and navigate away to your closest competitor?

Make sure your marketing strategy is thinking mobile first. Here are a few tips to ensure you have done this:

- Check all social media sites from your smartphone on a regular basis. Make sure the page's header image and other graphics look right on your phone.

- Use photos, graphics, and other images to break through the clutter. Remember, it is a tiny screen and text can be hard to read. Your posts need to catch their attention and be something they want to share!

- Pin the important stuff to the top. Both Facebook and Twitter allow stories to be pinned prominently to the top of a page. Showcase important events, but remember to change them periodically!

- Use video everywhere you can. Movement helps catch attention. If you can upload them directly to the site, do it!

- Maximize your *free* billboard. All of the social media sites have cover images. Make sure to change yours frequently and include your promotions, incentives and a Call to Action.

Learn to think mobile first. More and more people are looking at social sites from their phones; in fact most of us even get our news on social media. What do you do first thing each morning? I grab my phone; look at text messages, email and social media before I even get out of bed most days.

Facebook realized the importance of mobile years ago and started the transition away from desktop computers in 2012. Now, in 2017, that transition is mostly complete. And by 2020, eMarketer predicted in a Contently article[2] that 59 percent of U.S. Facebook users will only access the site via mobile. A hefty 80 percent of Facebook's revenue comes from mobile ads already.

Mobile is the future of business, and it is here now. Make sure you evaluate your mobile presence and get it up to speed.

THE IMPORTANCE OF VISUALS

In Chapter 1, we cited information from a ViaSearch new home buyers' survey that states 75–80 percent of new home buyers indicated that interactive visuals are very important to extremely important in the home shopping process. These include informational videos, virtual reality, and 3D tours.

Videos

There is no doubt that videos are created and watched—*a lot*. YouTube is often cited and the world's second largest search engine next to Google. Here are some recent stats taken from YouTube[3].

- YouTube has over a billion users.

- A billion hours of video are watched on YouTube each day.

- YouTube reaches more 18–34 and 18–49-year-olds than any cable network in the U.S.

- More than half of YouTube views come from mobile devices.

- 88 countries have YouTube local versions.

- YouTube can be navigated in 76 different languages (95 percent of the internet population).

A Contently article[4] states that videos are one of the three most important trends in social media in 2017. It supports this with information on how Facebook intends to transform to a "video first" platform. Facebook has already made huge strides with video including the introduction of Facebook Live, hosting videos on Facebook, and the new Facebook camera on mobile. Facebook employees are even quoted as saying "the camera is the keyboard." This really emphasizes the importance of video and photography as a platform. Conduct your own research—just ask any member of Generation Z what their preferred social media platforms are and why. The typical response is going to be Snapchat and Instagram.

Snapchat calls itself a "camera company" not a social network. According to Barron's Next[5], that isn't because it plans to compete with Cannon, GoPro, or Nikon, it is because Snapchat wants investors to understand that smartphone cameras play a key role in its business.

Twitter, Pinterest, and LinkedIn have all integrated video into their platforms as well. Twitter includes a live streaming video platform, as well as a video publisher.

Not only can you pin video to boards on Pinterest, but the photo-driven site now offers Promoted Video ads that fully play videos with sound. They are rather expensive starting at a minimum buy of $500,000, but they allow brands to display six Buyable Pins beneath each video as it plays.

Still not convinced? Here are a few more stats from Animoto[6].

- Four times as many consumers would rather watch a video about a product than read about it.

- One in four consumers actually *lose interest* in a company if it doesn't have video.

- Customers are nearly 50 percent more likely to read email newsletters that include links to video.

- Four out of five consumers say a video showing how a product or service works is important.

Consumers are watching more videos than ever. If you have not added video to the marketing mix, you need to put it on your To Do list!

The quality of the video produced is important as well. For a video that is going to go on your website, it should be professional. No one wants to watch a shaky video of a model home tour or their potential new home community. It is, however, perfectly acceptable to shoot user-generated video via Facebook Live or another platform at Open Houses, events, and for videos that are shot off the cuff.

Photos

Visuals and photos have tremendous power. Look how popular memes and GIFs are. Admit it, you laughed at a Trump or Hillary meme at some point, right?

Content is still king, but keep in mind that content is not only words or text, it is also visuals, video, graphics, infographics, and anything else used to present information.

An article in Medium[7] includes some great information. A picture is still worth a thousand words—if you have the right pictures. That usually means original pictures that are high quality and engaging—not a stock photo. Most people recognize stock photos now and it lowers the company's level of believability. Images should also be free of distractions such as dumpsters, tall grass, unrelated signage, workers, ladders, etc. Even better is to get your happy customers or raving fans to create user-generated content for you.

Ask your customers to post photos of themselves using your product or service and to post them to your Facebook, Instagram, Pinterest, or Twitter using a specific hashtag that relates to your company. This could be as part of a specific contest, or just part of your ongoing promotions strategy. Search #starbucks or #starbuckscoffee on Instagram and Twitter for an example of raving fans! These real photos, taken by real people, have an impact on engagement and interaction because they increase believability and give your company third party credibility. Your audience is looking for social proof of your offer, and seeing a friend post photos is an implied endorsement. Start building a library of user-generated images. It is pretty easy to do this today. Just ask your audience to participate.

According to Wikipedia[8] the average attention span of a human is less than eight seconds. Companies don't have much time to catch people's attention and images are one way to capture attention quickly. Because the human brain processes images 60,000 times quicker than text, there is a very compelling case to use eye catching graphics to break through the clutter and noise on social media. Consider using a mix of photos and images including professional photos, photos taken on a smart phone, Canva graphics, infographics and more. By mixing them up, you are more likely to present something that your audience can relate to, as well as keep their interest. Remember you have only eight seconds!

There are all sorts of studies on eye movement and how the eye is drawn to images and interprets them. Understanding a little about this can maximize the return on investment your business gets from images. For example happy images that include material symbols of success (like a new car or a new home) impact the emotions of followers that see them. Happy people in photos certainly make you want to smile and read the headline or article to see what they are celebrating.

Seemingly little things, like the direction people are facing in a photo, can impact time on site. If they are gazing off the page—whether it is a web page or a magazine page—they are taking the focus of the audience away from the very thing you want them to see. The people in the picture need to face the Call to Action or the most important thing on that page to get the absolute best results.

Using the right images on social media will help your company build brand, get attention, increase engagement, and stand out from the crowd.

Graphics

Graphics have become so important in social media that several free sites have spawned to take care of the demand for graphics. Among them are Canva, Pablo, PiktoChart, Recite, ImgFlip, PicMonkey, Quotes Cover, BeFunky, Over, Snappa and Adobe Spark. These sites provide for easy creation of quotes, photos with text, banners, header images and much, much more.

THE HASHTAG EXPLAINED

The # symbol is called a hashtag in social media. For those GenX and Boomers reading this, we called the # a pound sign back in the day. The Millennials and GenZ have never heard it called anything other than a hashtag, unless maybe they took keyboarding in school. (Oh and yes, we called that typing!) Like many industries, social media has developed a vocabulary of its own. Posts on Twitter are called tweets. Other fun words include feed, trending, flash mob, geo-target, force magnifier, native site, and user-generated content.

All of these words can be confusing for those who don't use social media on a daily basis; however, I get the most questions by far on hashtags. People wonder what on Earth they are and how to use them.

Hashtags were birthed way back in the early days of social media (2007). There wasn't a way to categorize or group content on Twitter, so someone came up with the idea of using the hashtag with a word or phrase strung together to make the site more searchable. Twitter users simply tweet their post with a #hashtag somewhere in the tweet. Then, other Twitter users would in turn use the same hashtag, or search for that hashtag. It is common to create a hashag for an incentive, promotion, particular subject, event, or conference. For instance the International Builders' Show uses #IBSVegas or #IBSOrlando depending on what city the show is in.

Hashtags are still commonly utilized on Twitter; however, the site is searchable without them. Once you hashtag a word in a post, if the social media account where the hashtag was used is open to the public, anyone can search your hashtag and find your content.

Like many things on social media, hashtags have evolved to span multiple sites and social media platforms. They are found on Facebook, Twitter, Instagram, Pinterest, and Google+. It is most common to see them used in posts on Twitter and Instagram. However, they are commonly used in contests and promotions on all sites.

To incorporate hashtags into posts, you should be well-versed in best practices. And, each site has slightly different acceptable uses. As a general rule, it is okay to tag or include one to three hashtags per post or tweet. On Twitter and Instagram, it is acceptable and even expected that every post will have a hashtag, or two, or three or 10. In fact, some research shows that to increase post engagement on Twitter, each post should contain no less than 10 or 11 hashtags.

These same 10 or 11 hashtags would look spammy if used in a post on Facebook, Pinterest, or Google+. Overuse of hashtags can interfere with the consumer's ability to read your content or even notice the Call to Action. Make sure that posts don't include so many hashtags that they completely distract readers from clicking through to your website. Hashtags need to enhance content, not distract from the message. Incorporate hashtags in your tweets that have potential to go viral. However, don't be a spammer and use trending hashtags that aren't relevant just to gain attention as it will backfire.

To properly use a hashtag, place it in front of the word or phrase and remove all of the spaces. For instance #photooftheday or #tagforlikes. You can even use upper and lower case letters in a hashtag to increase readability: #NameofBuilderShowcaseHome.

Here are some ideas on how you can put hashtags to work in the social media program for your business.

- **Trending topics**. Visit the native version of Twitter to see a list of trending hashtags. Incorporating these popular hashtags into your posts can boost that post's reach. Just make sure that your use of them is relevant.

- **Custom hashtags.** When conducting a contest, the creation of a custom hashtag can help contest organizers see all the people participating in the contest. For instance, a contest we ran last summer used #DenimSummerContest. A search for this hashtag will return results of posts we put online as well as contestants. Always search the hashtag you plan to use before announcing it or using it in promotional materials—you don't want to be caught off-guard or be surprised about who else is using it, or how it is used. And, always get a few different people to look at the hashtag to make sure it doesn't say anything that you have not noticed.

- **Find and follow people.** Want to find all the #painters or #builders or #realtors in a specific area? Search those hashtags or ones they might be using to find your audience and then start interacting with them.

- **Public opinions and events.** Many people employ a second screen while they watch TV. This means that they use a smartphone, tablet, or laptop to enhance their TV watching experience. Just watch for trending hashtags while the Emmys, Oscars, or Grammys are on and chime in.

- **Customer service.** Consumers use social media to get solutions to their customer service problems. Examples of this can be found by looking at any of the airlines accounts or any of the cable or high speed network providers. Your business needs to keep an eye on hashtags to see if anyone is blowing it up for customer service.

Hashtags are used commonly in social media, and there is a lot of information on the internet about them. Search for hashtags and you'll find lots of cool sites. One that tracks hashtags is www.hashtags.org. Hashtags can be registered and searched here. Just enter a specific hashtag in the blank at the top of the site to discover it has trended over 24 hours.

FACEBOOK 6

Now that you have an idea on how to put a social media program together, let's dive into each social media site. I'll share information about the site, how to use it for your business, some cool functionality of the site and what you should definitely be using. A lot of social sites are covered in this book. Don't feel like you need to use all of them to that a successful social media program. Your program can be successful with just two or three social sites, a blog, and a website if your marketing strategy creates the necessary synergy between all of the marketing tactics.

Facebook is perhaps the social media platform that defines social media platforms. Surpassing two billion users in June of 2017, Facebook enjoys far better market saturation than any other outlet. With 79 percent of America's online adults on Facebook, it is *the* place businesses need to be to reach potential buyers.

Facebook users can post status updates, videos, and photos on their timelines. They can also share and comment on posts by their "friends" (people who have agreed to both share their information with the user and who see the user's information) or people they follow (people whose information they see but with whom they have not also agreed to share). Users can also react to posts with a variety of responses, from the original "like" button to newer emojis that range from love and laughter to sadness. (Much to the disappointment of many users, there is currently no "hate" reaction.)

Businesses on Facebook set up a "page," which is public by default. The business category determines the type of information that will be displayed on the page. For example, Facebook will prompt a business that identifies as "local" to enter an address, phone number and price range. A business that identifies as a "brand" will provide information on company history and available products. Users can like a business page, follow it, and share, comment on and react to posts. When a user responds to a business page in any way, that information is shared with the user's friends and followers. In this way, Facebook transforms consumers' purchase decisions into social transactions with the potential to expand a business's reach exponentially.

The vast amount of participation on Facebook makes it the optimal "push and pull" site in any marketing campaign. Ads, compelling content (including photos and video), and contests or promotions can entice users to engage—pulling them in to the business Facebook page and, preferably, over to a website, blog, or even a sales center. Once potential buyers are "pulled" in, businesses have an engaged audience and can "push" out targeted messaging.

WHO USES FACEBOOK?

- 2.01 billion monthly active users[1]

- 1.66 billion monthly active mobile users (1.57 billion mobile daily users)[2]

- 55 million status updates each day[3]

- 4,000 photos uploaded each second[4]

- Facebook users are 53 percent female and 47 percent male[5]

- More than 40 million active small business pages[6]

- The average user has 155 "friends"[7]

- The "like" button has been pressed 11.3 trillion times[8]

- The average amount of time spent per session is 20 minutes, equaling 600 hours per month[9]

- The average user is connected to 80 pages, events and groups[10]

- 66 percent of all users return daily[11]

- 79 percent of American adults who are online have Facebook pages[12]

- 26 percent of accounts are with people in the 25–34 age group, 19 percent by 35–44 age group, 18 percent by 18–24 age group, 17 percent by 55+ group, and 16 percent by 44–55 age group[13].

BASIC FEATURES AND TOOLS TO USE FOR BUSINESS

Business Page. As discussed above, a "page" is a business's primary presence on Facebook. Before sharing a page, upload the appropriate images (cover photo and profile photo), complete the About Us section, and get started with posts before inviting friends and customers to like and interact. The cover photo is the billboard type image that appears at the top of the page. Make sure to change your cover photo often—at least quarterly, if not monthly. Take advantage of the option to add a Call to Action button below the bottom righthand corner of the cover photo, encouraging visitors to call or view your website. Update your page regularly with status updates, photos and video. Include a mix of messages. Consumers don't want to be "sold to" with every update. Find ways to educate them and to incorporate humor.

Customer support. Creating a business page automatically enables Facebook Messenger for your business. This allows customers, fans, and potential customers to contact your business privately. This also enables you to remove discussions of customer comments or complaints from public view. Show a public response by responding appropriately and offering to continue the conversation privately, then message the customer. This way, the public knows the business is responsive, but the details of continuing conversation remain confidential.

Groups. Facebook Groups bring together people who share a common interest. Group members can see and interact with posts, which will appear in their news feeds. A private group—with membership by invitation only—might be a good option for communicating with neighbors in a new home community or for your HBA, SMC, or PWB, for example. Industry groups can help build relationships among peers.

Facebook Live. Live video streaming is a relatively new Facebook feature that promises great rewards for businesses. Already, studies have shown that live streams encourage three times more engagement than other videos[14]. When a live stream begins, all followers receive an immediate notification—and, at present this is the only way to connect instantly with all followers. Live videos should last at least eight to 10 minutes or longer, as it may take some time before notified followers join in. Viewers can comment and react during a live stream, so it's important to acknowledge those viewers and answer questions as they come in. After the live stream, you can save the video to your page and use the embed code to include it in your website or blog. Ideas for live videos include homebuyer or Realtor events, model home openings or tours, question and answers with the experts, or a behind-the-scenes look at a building site or design center.

Cross promotion. Facebook tools allow you to bring people in or send people out to other sites. Include Facebook sharing on your website or blog to encourage readers to share content from your sites on their own Facebook timelines. Add social media information, such as a Pinterest icon, on your Facebook page to direct people to your other social media channels. Embed videos or posts on your website or blog.

Videos and photos. We've already discussed the importance of videos and photos in social media. While live streaming and iPhone snapshots will keep your posts fun and entertaining, a healthy mix of professional video and photography is important in maintaining your brand as well. Facebook now accepts 360-degree videos and photos, an option that is popular with homebuyers. You can create the photos using a panoramic shot of a home, though you will need special cameras to create a 360-degree video.

ADVERTISING

From promoting a post to running a video ad, Facebook offers a variety of options to meet various marketing goals and budget requirements. Some of the more interesting tools available to advertisers are those used to target specific audiences. For example, in a retargeting campaign, you can embed a Facebook pixel on your website, then advertise to Facebook users who have visited your site. By uploading your email list, you can target those you already have in your database who are also Facebook users. As on other social media sites, ads can also target certain demographics, geographic areas and people who have shown particular interests through their online activity. Careful audience selection creates a more efficient use of advertising dollars.

FACEBOOK SCORECARD

- Is your Facebook page complete, with all About Us information included, a cover photo with a Call to Action (CTA) button and several posts?

- Have you used Facebook Live to stream an event or Q&A session?

- Have you included the Facebook share button on your blog or website?

- Have you embedded any videos, images, or posts from your Facebook page into your website or blog?

- Are you regularly interacting with your followers and responding to inquiries in a timely manner on other professionals' pages?

- Are you making timely posts?

FACEBOOK CHEAT SHEET

- Maximize your Facebook presence. Make sure you have completed all of the basic About Us information, loaded a cover photo, added a CTA button and posted. You don't want fans coming to an empty page.

- Use Facebook Live! It is the only way you can message all of your followers all at once!

- Make it easy for your fans to share your content by including the Facebook share button on your website or blog.

- Once you have Facebook Live videos, include them on you blog or website.

- Facebook gives you a rating based on how fast you respond to inquiries through Facebook Messenger. So, respond fast for a good rating!

- While different audiences may vary, posts that receive the most engagement are generally made toward the end of the week (Wednesday through Sunday) and in the afternoon or evening hours. Posts made early morning, late at night or anytime on a Monday or Tuesday are generally not reacted to, commented on or shared by as many people.

TWITTER 7

As one of the old-timers in today's social media landscape, Twitter may seem passé to you. In terms of growth, many would agree. Despite the platform's prominent role in the national political media, investors were disappointed when the number of monthly active users did not grow at all in the second quarter of 2017. Though the company is quick to note that the number of daily active users increased by 12 percent during that time, it does not release specific numbers[1]. Showing how hard numbers are to come by for Twitter, a different source that said daily active users were up 14 percent and that the company was experiencing its 4th consecutive quarter of growth[2].

Despite concerns of stagnation, I urge you to continue including Twitter as a valuable component of your social media marketing. Not only are the usage statistics still impressive (see "Who uses Twitter" below), but there are several differentiating factors that make the platform relevant.

First, users are open to learning about businesses and are motivated to buy. According to a survey sponsored by Twitter[3], 93.3 percent of users who follow a small or medium sized business plan to make a purchase, and 66.4 percent have discovered a new small or medium business on Twitter. After discovering a business on Twitter, 73.4 percent have followed the business, and about a third have engaged by retweeting or directing a tweet to the company. Advertising helps businesses gain followers, too. Of those surveyed who are following a small or medium sized business, 85.4 percent say that promotional ads helped them discover a business, and 68 percent say they have followed a business after noticing an ad.

Second, of the mainstream social media platforms, Twitter stands out as being more popular with men than with women. If you're looking for a place to showcase the enviable man caves, smart home components, and media rooms that set your homes apart, you're likely to find an audience here that's ready to listen. If you're building low-maintenance or no-maintenance communities, the guys out there are likely to be intrigued. After all, they would rather spend their weekends doing something other than lawn work.

Third, Twitter allows you to follow and interact with people who have not accepted a request from you. If you see conversations happening about a topic that is relevant to your company, you can jump in. You can follow all the top local Realtors and start engaging with them.

Finally, and perhaps the most important in terms of your overall marketing picture, users who arrive on a company website through Twitter typically spend more time there than those that discover sites through other platforms. Though your Tweet is limited in length, including a hyperlink to your website is a good way to offer more complete information and turn followers into customers. Make sure to look at your social media traffic in Google Analytics to determine which sites sent the best quality traffic.

WHO USES TWITTER?

Let's take a look at some Twitter statistics[4]:

- 67 million people in the U.S. are on Twitter.

- 37 percent of users are between the ages of 18–29 and 25 percent are between 30 and 49.

- 54 percent of users earn more than $50,000 a year.

- 500 million tweets are sent each day.

- 328 million monthly active users as of August 2017

- 100 million daily active users as of January 2017

- 24 percent of male internet users and 21 percent of female internet users are on Twitter.

BASIC FEATURES AND TOOLS
TO USE FOR BUSINESS

Let's review Twitter's lingo. Users post updates of up to 140 characters, called tweets. (Note that in September 2017 Twitter started testing tweets of up to 280 characters with a limited number of users. It is unclear when this will be rolled out to all Twitter users, but there are a lot of browser extensions and work arounds if you want to Tweet with 280 characters now). Links, videos, photos, and GIFs can be included and do not count in your character limit. The company reports that people are three times more likely to engage with tweets that have videos and photos[5], so take full advantage of the opportunity. You can include up to four photos with each tweet.

You can share, or Retweet, someone else's post. You can also reply and like a tweet. A "mention" is when you include a person's username preceded by the @ symbol to draw their attention to a Tweet. You can also send private messages via twitter to other users.

As discussed in Chapter 5, a social media standard that started on Twitter is the use of the hashtag to link information on a given topic. By typing the # sign followed by a word or phrase related to your topic (eliminate all spaces), it makes it easier for other Twitter users to find your post. On your own Twitter Home page, you can organize tweets according to hashtags. For example, you can search "#homebuilder." If any Twitter user employs that hashtag, it will appear grouped together in that search. If you see a hashtag of interest in your feed, you can click on it to search for other Tweets related to that topic. Popular hashtags are highlighted as Trending Topics.

Custom Timelines, a feature offered by TweetDeck, allow companies and individuals to group a set of tweets together by user, hashtag or keyword. So, in essence, you customize your Twitter stream to what you want to see whether that is a stream on diving at the Olympics, or one on a specific trending topic. These timelines are public and have their own page on Twitter. They are also sharable and can be embedded onto websites.

There are a multitude of ways that businesses can use Twitter Custom Timelines to promote their products and services. Here are a few that we have seen:

- Campaign promotion
- Sharing testimonials
- Live event management
- Live Q&A sessions

It is common for businesses to solicit and respond to customer feedback on Twitter. A special name, such as @MyCompanyNameCustomer may be the perfect channel for you to accept comments from customers. When the positive comments role in, you can respond quickly with thanks, likes, and retweets as appropriate. If you receive negative feedback, a fast and professional response can counter any negative results. At a minimum, acknowledge the negative feedback publicly along with a promise to address it. If you want to invite the customer into a private conversation via direct message, so the conversation is no longer public, you will both need to follow each other. Another option is to send them a direct link to your online chat or warranty service request form.

One way to make Twitter more manageable is the ability to pre-schedule and manage tweets through TweetDeck, Hootsuite, or SocialJukebox (formerly TweetJukebox). A potential drawback to using these services and prescheduling your tweets is that you may inadvertently miss out on the conversations that arise and relationships that develop when you actively engage and respond to others communicating on the same topics. You'll get your best results from combining some automation with lots of old-fashioned conversation—well, old-fashioned in Twitter terms.

ADVERTISING

You may wish to advertise on Twitter to raise your profile. According to the company, ad engagements increased 151 percent in 2016 over the previous year, while advertising costs actually fell 21 percent per engagement for Q4 of 2016[6]. If your goal is to attract more followers, you can create a Followers campaign, which promotes your business in targeted users' Home timelines and in their "Who to follow" panel. A Quick Promote campaign is a way to draw attention to a particular tweet. The campaign promotes the targeted tweet to users in the geographic area you specify and with users who are likely to be interested in the interested in the topic. You can see results at any time by clicking on "See Tweet Activity" below the tweet. You might consider Quick Promote on tweets that are proving to be particularly engaging with your followers, on important announcements, and to advertise events.

It is very hard to find what advertising on Twitter costs. According to ThriveHive[7], ad costs range from $1.35 per engagement to $200,000 to be included in the Promoted Trends.

Twitter Scorecard

- Are tweets are made daily or regularly?

- Is content is engaging and informational?

- Are hashtags are incorporated into tweets?

- Does the page engage with others by replying to tweets, and interacting?

- Do the company logo, colors, and fonts match the logo used on the website?

- Is a custom banner header uploaded and changed frequently?

- Has an important tweet been pinned to the top of the timeline?

Twitter Cheat Sheet

- Pages can tweet incessantly and not offend anyone. Queue up your TweetDeck and send 5, 10, or 20 tweets a day.

- If your content is boring, try to jazz it up. What you say needs to have personality. Consider adding polls as a way to get interaction.

- Hashtags will help people to find you and thus improve your following.

- Make sure your account is not standing in the corner at a cocktail party pushing marketing messages. Find a few relevant accounts (partners, vendors) to retweet and engage with.

- This is a good time to make sure all corporate branding is consistent across all of your social media accounts.

- The custom banner header is a free billboard. Promote your upcoming event. Change it monthly or quarterly. Take full advantage of this.

- Pin your most important news or announcements to the top of your Twitter page. Share your news, make sure people don't miss it!

GOOGLE+ AND
GOOGLE MY BUSINESS

Google+, launched in June 2011, is Google's fourth attempt at social networking. Previous sites include Google Buzz, Google Friend Connect, and Orkut. Although the site is viewed as a social network, its power is actually its ability to help with search engine optimization. The growth of Google+ has been slow. Perhaps this is because Google first called the site a social network and later revised this description to call it a social layer across all of Google's services.

Google+ allows people and pages to have accounts. They can post status updates with photos or videos to the stream. The site allows users to group relationships into various categories called circles (versus just having friends). Other functionality includes hangouts (text and video chat), location tagging and more.

Google My Business is sometimes confused with Google+. Google My Business provides businesses with a free business listing on Google and the ability to be included in Google Maps and thus local search. By posting regularly to Google My Business you can keep your customers coming back to see what is new.

Before we start talking about the value of Google+ and Google My Business as social media platforms, consider these two visible results of establishing an account:

1 · When someone uses Google to search for your business name, a sidebar will appear on the right side of the screen. Your Google My Business account will be used to populate the information. If you do not have an account, the information may be inaccurate or incomplete. Google My Business ensures facts like your business hours and contact information

are correct. You can also add photos and update it regularly with new information. Customer reviews also show up here, so it is important to refer back to Chapter 5 Reputation Management!

2 · Google immediately indexes everything you share on Google+. Your posts will have a higher potential to show up in search results, giving your company more visibility. Why? Well, it is simple, Google owns Google+, so if you post links to your blog posts and your website on your Google+ page, this alerts the Google bot to go look at them. This gets these pages indexed by Google much more quickly.

Still not convinced? While the numbers of people who use Google+ regularly may pale in comparison to Facebook usage, the platform had 111 million active users in 2017[1]. It is very hard to get good stats on Google+ usage because Google does not seem to release these. However, Google+ technically has more users than Facebook, as the site has 2.5 billion profiles. But a quick look informs us that many of these profiles were set up in order to access Google My Business or by default because they have a Google login for some service. An estimated 30 percent of smartphone users visit the site once a month. And, 77 percent of searches originate on Google[2].

WHO USES GOOGLE+?

The statistics for this site are all over the place. While our earlier research shows that Google+ had 111 million active users in 2017 with 2.5 billion profiles, this research from Statistic Brain[3] reports the following:

- 395 million active users

- 34 million unique monthly visits

- 28 percent of users are age 15–34

- 26 percent female, 73 percent male

- 40 percent of marketers use Google+

- 70 percent of businesses use Google+

- Average time per visit: 3:46

- 30 percent of smartphone users visit the site at least once a month.

Google+ behaves like other social media platforms. You can offer status updates or share images, articles and videos. A "like" in the Google+ world is called a "+1." To get started, set up a Gmail address with Google. Like other social media platforms, best practice is to vary the types of content you create and share. Target your content to different audiences by organizing your contacts into Circles, or categorized lists. Think about creating Circles of Realtor contacts, lender contacts and vendor contacts, for example.

Through a Google+ account, you can start Collections of content, to which you alone can post and share. Consider starting or join a Community, or Group. Any member of a Community can share among its members, and there's no limit to the number of members. If a Community you join is only tangentially related to your business, you can still raise awareness of your company and establish yourself as an expert by chiming in if someone asks a question or posts content relevant to you.

When users log in to Google+, they see suggested topics. Users can explore these topic areas to discover new Communities, Collections, and users who may share their own interests.

BASIC FEATURES AND TOOLS TO USE FOR BUSINESS

Home Stream. This is where you go to see all the posts that people have shared. (In Facebook terms, this would be called your wall.) Once you follow profiles of other users and Collections and Communities, you will start to see information that is of more interest to you. From your home stream you can +1 (like) it, comment on it or reshare it. If you want people to like your page and your content, you should like some of theirs!

Following. You should find and follow people, pages, Collections, and Communities. You can follow people without them having to accept you. In other words, you can follow them and see their content and they don't have to follow you back. They won't see your content if they don't follow you—their loss, right?

Collections. This is a neat feature that offers lots of opportunities for businesses. You can create Collections based on interests, so why not create a Collection of remodeling ideas? Or a collection for each of your new home communities? Collections can even be created privately so that only certain people can see them. When you create a Collection you can choose whether it will be open to the public or who will see it. When people follow your Collection they will see it in their home stream and they can choose whether they get notifications on the Collection.

Collection versus Community. So, what the heck is the difference between a Collection and a Community? Collections are managed by one person or company and they are the only ones that can post to it. Communities can have more than one owner or manager, and other people can join. Everyone that is a member of that Community can post their updates to the Community.

Photo and video settings. You can turn the geolocation for photos on to default on or off. And you can choose whether people can download the photos and videos you share. . . or not.

Posting. When you update your status by posting and share it with the public, anyone can see it whether they are on Google+ or not. Your post might even show up in searches (woot woot). You can have conversations about content on the site by commenting on posts. If you see a post you like, you can +1 it, reshare it to your own stream, Collection, or Community. Remember, you can filter your updates to cause an update or photo to only show up in certain cities or only to certain circles.

GOOGLE+ SCORECARD

- Do you have a check mark on your Google+ page showing that it is verified? Do you have a Google My Business listing?

- Do you post regularly? When was the last time you posted? Was it a year ago? Yikes!

- Have you started a Collection or joined a Community?

- Is your branding on Google+ consistent with your website and collateral? Is the logo the same and sized appropriately? Do the colors match?

- Have you personalized your page with a custom header?

- Do you interact with other? Have you followed other businesses and users? Do you share, comment, and +1 their posts?

- Have any of your happy buyers written a review?

- Do your posts link back to your company's website or blog?

GOOGLE+ CHEAT SHEET

- Verify your business on Google+. Get a check mark on your Google+ page and show better results in Google Maps, searches and all things Google by creating a Google My Business listing (or gain access if your listing has already been created). Google will cross-examine information you provide with other directories (think Yellow Pages or Yelp) to confirm the information is consistent. When it all looks accurate, Google is more likely to rank your company higher in search engine results pages (SERPs).

- Create a social media strategy for how often you are going to post. A content calendar will help keep you on track for a few posts a month.

- Start a Collection featuring your homes, community, products, most recent remodel, etc., and join a few Communities. This will help your page get noticed more.

- Remain consistent in your branding. The colors, artwork and language you use in Google+ should match the colors and logo on your website, blog and other social media channels.

- Personalize your page. Give users a glimpse of your employees, offices, and events. This will help to establish a relationship with your followers (and potential buyers).

- Interact. Follow other businesses and users. Share, comment and +1 their posts. Employ the + symbol to tag others as you would in other social media platforms. People and businesses like to be noticed. (Plus, every time you interact, you send data back to Google that says you are an active company that deserves to be ranked well in search engine results.)

- Encourage reviews. When you're soliciting customer feedback, encourage them to leave reviews by going to the About section of your Google account. These reviews will populate in your Google results.

- Drive traffic. Remember to include links back to your company's website or blog in all posts.

LINKEDIN 9

Linkedln, launched in May 2003, is a social networking site focused on business- and employment-oriented social networking. To this end, most of the networking that occurs on the site is professional in nature—companies posting jobs, and job seekers posting their resumes. The site, based in the United States, is available in 24 languages including French, Chinese, German, Italian, and many others. For the past several years the site's monetization has come from recruiters and businesses purchasing information on members and using this information to help them fill positions. LinkedIn was purchased by Microsoft in 2016 for $26.4 billion.

LinkedIn users create profiles and connect to each other. Companies can create pages that users can follow. Many of the relationships on the site mimic relationships that business professionals have in real life.

WHO USES LINKEDIN?

In April 2017, LinkedIn reported reaching 500 million users in more than 200 countries[1]. The company doesn't report the number of active users who log in at least monthly, and estimates vary. Apptopia, a company that provides intelligence and statistics on mobile apps, estimated 260 million monthly users in March 2017[2]. VentureBeat estimated that 25 percent of users, or 125 million, actively visit the site each month[3]. A Pew Research Center report released in January 2017 stated that 18 percent of LinkedIn users visit the site daily, 31 percent weekly and 51 percent less frequently[4].

I contend that LinkedIn offers a variety of benefits for your business and your overall marketing plan. First, even relatively inactive users can make introductions and share your content. According to LinkedIn, each connection you created on the site represents an average of 400 people you could get introduced to or build a relationship with. And these are strong connections. A National Association of Realtors study found the average age of a homebuyer in 2016 was 44 years, the same it had been for three years. Of all U.S. adults ages 30–49, a third of them are on LinkedIn. All social media sites lag behind Facebook in this area, of course, and LinkedIn is slightly behind Pinterest (32 percent) and tied with Instagram (31 percent). However, LinkedIn brings two additional demographics that will be appealing to home builders—the largest percentage of U.S. adults with incomes of at least $75,000 (45 percent) and the largest percentage of college graduates (49 percent)[5].

Like many social media sites, the statistics for LinkedIn are all over the place. Here is a quick list from Omnicore Agency[6]:

- 467 million active users

- 106 million unique monthly users

- 40 percent of users use the site daily

- 13 percent of users are age 15–34

- 44 percent female, 57 percent male

- 44 percent of LinkedIn users earn more than $75,000 a year

- 40 million students and recent college graduates are on the site.

WHAT IS LINKEDIN?

Of all the social media sites we're discussing, you may consider LinkedIn the least "social." On a personal level, the site for many is more about keeping an online resume than building the types of relationships seen in traditional social media. And who goes to LinkedIn looking to buy a product? If you're not looking to hire someone, and you're not in the job market yourself, why bother with LinkedIn?

So, on LinkedIn, users are less likely to happen across your content as they are on other sites they visit more frequently. How does LinkedIn remain relevant when you're selling homes?

The platform offers a unique opportunity to build relationships and strengthen your professional reputation with real estate agents, vendors, and other professionals with whom you interact. To this end, it's important to share and publish content that establishes you as an expert and industry leader and to reciprocate when your connections share content or updates. Remember, even your business connections live somewhere. By supporting their professional endeavors online, you may be creating future customers at the same time you're strengthening business relationships.

Perhaps most important to your overall social media marketing success, is to use LinkedIn as an excellent means of syndicating your blog content. By posting portions of your articles with a link back to your blog posts on LinkedIn, you have another outlet for gaining traction, growing traffic to your website, and building your SEO.

LinkedIn is the perfect platform for sharing professional information like an upcoming education event, open house, new community, or your recent big promotion. Sharing this information on LinkedIn is a great way to share company news in a quieter, less-cluttered environment. Even if your followers and connections don't log into LinkedIn frequently, they still receive regular email updates from the platform. If you consistently provide interesting and useful information, they will pay attention when those email updates pertain to you.

Another way I use LinkedIn regularly is for research. If I'm meeting someone new, whether a vendor or potential client, I'll use LinkedIn to prepare for an in-person conversation. Learning more about a person's professional and educational background helps me identify commonalities before we ever meet in person. This little bit of extra knowledge, which is appropriate for a professional relationship, has made the "getting to know you" small talk flow seamlessly in many meetings.

BASIC FEATURES AND TOOLS TO USE FOR BUSINESS

LinkedIn is similar to Facebook in that users can connect with other people and follow companies and organizations. A primary difference is that the connections and content are usually based on professional interests rather than purely social ones.

Users can "like" and comment on posts to build relationships, and also join groups related to topics of interest. For example, if you want to get news from the marketing field, you might join a group for marketers. You may even find a narrower group of marketers in a specific industry, specializing in a specific medium, or even focused in a geographic area.

When you're selecting content to post to LinkedIn, here are some relatively new features you may want to try:

- **Write article and include multiple images in the article.** This may not seem like a big deal at first, but we've already discussed how important images are in Chapter 5. With the ability to include multiple images, you can break up and sustain interest in longer articles, post more pictures from your last charity work day, or even share the flyers for your new promotion.

- **Use video.** You can upload videos of up to 10 minutes to LinkedIn. This is a good feature if you want to share a sales team presentation, show off a new model home, or record a conference presentation. Eventually, you'll be able to record and post video from within the app, too. As of the writing of this book, LinkedIn reported that the feature would be launched to all users soon.

- **It doesn't matter if your target audiences aren't logging into LinkedIn every day.** They can now see your posts, videos, and articles even when logged out. You can copy your post's URL via the control menu and share it with friends on Facebook, Twitter, and around the web.

- **Share drafts.** Need some peer review of a post before you publish it? The article edit menu now has a "Share Draft" option. You grab the link and share it only with those you'd like to give a preview.

- **Comments.** You now have the option to enable or disable comments related to your posts and articles. This new control will allow you to maintain your brand personality and culture, even if commenters happen to act differently.

Companies on LinkedIn can promote their products and services via Company Pages. Here are some of our favorite ways to do this.

- **Complete your company profile.** *Hint:* the About section is searchable and indexed on Google so make sure to include all of your keywords here.

- **Post frequent company updates.** Include all of your company blog posts as updates with a brief overview of what the post is about and a link back to the website. Also share relevant industry articles, company news, videos and SlideShare presentations.

- **Create a Showcase Page(s) to highlight your products and services.** These are free pages designed to spotlighting a brand, business unit, or initiative. Create pages for aspects of your business that use distinct messaging and target specific audiences. Think about these as long-term branding initiatives, not just promotions. You can post updates to Showcase Pages as well as add video.

- **Upload multiple photos in a single post.** At present this tool is only available on iOS, but desktop and Android are coming soon. This allows you to showcase the most recent presentation you did, or multiple event photos. I'm sure you will come up with multiple uses for this!

- **Customize Pages for global audiences.** Company Pages and Showcase Pages can be set up in more than 20 languages. Then use filters like geography and language to target the audience for each update.

- **Share and share more.** Have a strategy for employees to share content from the Corporate Page to their personal page. The more people that share your content, the more people who will see it.

- **Make your content relevant to your primary audience.** True, anyone could come to look at your page, but since LinkedIn is geared to professional relationships, that's the type of messaging users of all kinds will expect to find. Post information that business-minded people will appreciate. Show them value so they will want to stay connected to your business.

- **Be responsive.** Take notice when people comment on and share your posts. Thank them and reciprocate when you can. Your responsiveness will help build the lasting relationships you're seeking.

ADVERTISING

I used to think of advertising on LinkedIn only in terms of companies looking for employees. That's only a small piece of the LinkedIn advertising puzzle. Sponsored Updates (articles that appear in a user's news feed) and ads (advertisements that appear on the right-hand column of the screen with graphics and text) can each drive traffic to your company's page. Choose your target audience, post relevant and interesting content, employ eye-catching images (no stock photos), and include a CTA to drive engagements. When users respond through comments, likes, or page visits, be sure to interact with them and build engagement.

Advertising rates are based on pay-per-click or impressions. With no long-term contracts, LinkedIn advertising can be a cost-effective way to drive traffic to your page and website.

LINKEDIN SCORECARD

- Does your Company Page have a logo and a cover image?

- Have you optimized the content in your About section? Remember this can be indexed by Google and other search engines.

- When was the last time you posted?

- Are you including multiple photos in your posts?

- Have you launched a Showcase Page?

LINKEDIN CHEAT SHEET

- Pages with logos get six times more views on LinkedIn. The cover image is like having a free billboard to catch attention. Don't pass on this opportunity!

- Because Google can crawl and index pages on LinkedIn, it is important to include keywords in the About section for your Company Page.

- Your business page should also remain current with a regular rotation of fresh content. Whether you're sharing company news, and industry insight, open job positions, or your blog post, consistency is important. Whether job seekers, industry partners, or potential customers visiting your page, show them your best face, not a blank page.

- Remember a picture is worth a thousand words. Catch their attention with a series of photos.

- Your Company Page should be informative. Show visitors and followers your products and services as well as your company culture by building out Showcase Pages.

PINTEREST 10

I f Facebook is about building relationships and Instagram is about sharing your life or brand through photos, Pinterest is about ideas, planning, and decision making.

Founded in 2010, the Pinterest is the third largest social media platform in the U.S., with 31 percent adoption among online Americans and 26 percent of all Americans[1]. Growth has been stable since 2015[2]. Usage is stronger among women, but male users grew 120 percent in 2015[3].

Pinterest is based on the concept of an old-fashioned pin board. Users collect online images, articles or other information by "pinning" them to boards they organize around their own topics of interest. Items they've pinned are shared with their followers. Users can also search for public pins they want to add to their own boards through a typical word search. Visual searches are also possible using the Lens function. Pinners focus the Lens on an image from a Pin or even their own camera to search for similar images across Pins.

"Pinners associate Pinterest with taking action," Pinterest staffer Gunner Johnson wrote on the company's blog in 2017. "98 percent of Pinners report trying new things they find on Pinterest compared to an average 71 percent across social media platforms. Before they even open the app, they intend to act[4]."

And these Pinterest-inspired actions are far more than trying new recipes or tackling DIY projects. Pinners use the site as a starting point for purchase decisions. Users are 47 percent more likely to have a major life event coming up within six months[5], and they welcome the influence of marketers. In fact, 83 percent say they prefer to follow a brand or store over a celebrity[6]. Of Millennial users, 47 percent have purchased something they have shared, compared with 9 percent of Facebook users and 14 percent of Twitter users[7].

Pinners generally start searching the site two to three months before a purchase[8]. In a 2015 survey of active Pinners, 96 percent used the site to gather information and conduct research; 93 percent sought help in planning for purchases; and 87 percent had used the site to help with them decide what to purchase[9]. It pays to get in front of Pinterest users as they start the buying process. The site has a higher ratio of converting first impressions (versus converting last impressions) out of all other social, digital and search platforms[10].

WHO USES PINTEREST?

- Pinterest has 150 million active users, including 70 million in the U.S.[11]

- 36 percent of Pinterest users are Millennials, followed very closely by Gen Xers (34 percent). Boomers lag behind at 18 percent[12].

- 66 percent of Pinterest users have an annual household income higher than $50,000, with 35 percent about the $75,000 mark[13].

- 25 percent of Pinners visit the site daily[14].

- Pinterest contains 74 billion ideas[15].

- Two-thirds of Pins showcase a brand or product[16].

- Pinners like to shop! They are 39 percent more likely to be active retail shoppers, and they spend 29 percent more than non-Pinners[17].

- Nearly 85 percent of all Pinterest searches are on mobile[18].

- Five percent of all referral traffic to websites is from Pinterest, second only to Facebook[19].

Women make most decisions related to homebuying, so I'm going to assume that one of your target audiences is women. This makes Pinterest the perfect site for your company as it is estimated that 81 percent of Pinners are female.

BASIC FEATURES AND TOOLS FOR BUSINESS

Build your profile. Be sure to fully build your profile with your company description, logo, contact information, and links to your website, blog, and other social media profiles.

Plan ahead. A little time strategizing your boards and the types of content they will contain can save significant time later. Rearranging your boards will become more difficult as you get more pins and more followers. You will want to avoid deleting boards later because you'll also lose that board's followers.

Build your brand...and stick with it. Showcase your products and services. The images and information you pin should be consistent with what you're selling. You may want to give your potential buyers something to dream about, but you also need to show them finishes available at your base prices. If they're seeing only upgrades on Pinterest, they will likely be surprised and disappointed when they see your spec sheet.

Build out your rotating showcase. Set up a selection of pins featuring your most popular pins or best ideas in a Pinterest rotating showcase. This will be the first thing that people notice when they come to you page as the movement attracts attention!

Help potential buyers visualize themselves in their new home and neighborhood. Share holiday decor, home design tips and entertaining ideas appropriate to the types of homes and communities you promote. For example, if you are selling townhomes, you might feature photos of intimate gatherings. Save pins about large, outdoor parties to target buyers in communities with more spacious home sites.

Recommended frequency of pinning. Deliberate, planned pinning will work better for you than sporadic, all-day pinning sprees. Try sharing no more than a few Pins at a time every few days.

Share company news. New floor designs? New community? New employees? New promotion? Pin it!

Promote events. Remember to pin about your agent events, ground breakings, and model home openings. Include pictures so buyers, agents and business partners will catch the excitement.

Create interaction. Fill boards with fun and useful content. Consider what you would like to see if you were your own customer, from something funny memes about the home buying process to helpful hints for making the move easier. Interact with other companies and boards, and they'll likely reciprocate.

Share photos. People like to see themselves and people they know in pictures. Photos of agents, vendors, business partners, and homebuyers also act as silent testimonials—even if the words aren't spelled out, the person's involvement with your brand serves as an endorsement.

Educate. Teach potential buyers what to expect. Once they have a contract on a new home, what is the build out process? When can they make selections? Will they have a final walk through? What can you tell them about the mortgage process? Infographics, educational videos and mortgage calculators keep your buyers informed before and during the process. They will appreciate the help.

Use infographics and word clouds. Infographics (visual interpretations of information) and word clouds (representations of groups of words in a graphic form) have become popular on Pinterest and other social networks. Graphics make otherwise dry statistics both more memorable and easier to comprehend quickly. You could create a word cloud of key words from buyer testimonials regarding your service or perhaps from your interior designers as they describe your homes.

You can be creative with your infographics as well. For an effective infographic:

- Start with relevant, accurate information.

- Show the most data near the top or in the center of the field.

- Eliminate visual and mental clutter. Include only the most interesting, topical data.

- Be imaginative with graphics that complement the type of information you're sharing.

- Above all, be clear!

Repurpose. Are you creating quality, visually-compelling content for other outlets? Of course you are! Think about blog posts, industry news, awards, market research, your company's vision board, links to vendors, partners, and other resources, and community involvement. All are appropriate for Pinterest, too.

Connect to Facebook. Integrate Pinterest into your bigger social media program by promoting your account on Facebook. You can post about your Pinterest boards and even add a Pinterest tab to your Facebook page. Cross posting is sort of like earning compound interest—the interaction builds on itself with little help from you.

Build Niche Boards. Remember that your boards do not need to be all things to all people. Some pinners will follow only a few or maybe even just one of your boards. Think about these pinners and create targeted boards with popular (and still relevant) themes that will introduce your brand to a new audience.

Videos. One benefit of sharing videos on Pinterest is that you choose how they will be ordered. You can create a highly-organized, visual package on Pinterest that drives people to your YouTube videos. You can make it easy to view all of your product videos and even put customer testimonial videos front and center. When you create your video board, be sure to add the word "video," "videos" or "video series" to your description, along with your company name and other keywords.

Timeless content. Social media, and media in general, focus on bringing you the latest news. While your Pinterest boards should be up-to-date, they also can provide your history and an overview of your products. Use boards to show a new home community's progression or present a history of home styles and finishes through the years. Gather photos of a model home, of all our different communities, or of all your home plans in one place.

Pin from your website or blog. If you upload photos and images directly from your hard drive or your camera, what will happen when visitors click on those images? They go nowhere. If you want Pinners to make it back to your website or blog, that's where you'll want to grab your content.

Categories, keywords, and descriptions. While visual search is available on Pinterest, most searches are completed with words or phrases. It's important to provide accurate descriptions, assign logical categories, and integrate appropriate keywords.

Be careful with repins. You'll want most of your Pins to be original. It's okay to repin when the content is relevant and supports your brand. Repinning your vendors' and preferred partners' posts strategically can build relationships, and that's what social media is all about.

ADVERTISING

Promoted Pins are the typical way to invest your advertising dollars in Pinterest. Save a Promoted Pin and choose an audience to target and agree to pay for each engagement (closeup, repin, or click). When a user saves your Promoted Pin, other users will see it in their feeds as well, providing additional exposure to potential buyers. Promoted pins are not marked as advertisements and do not interfere with the Pinner's experience.

Engagement rates for Promoted Pins are typically two- to five percent higher than the industry average. You may not be paying to promote them long-term, but Pins last forever. Your promoted Pin appears in more places and continues to engage people (and drive them to your website) for years to come. According to Pinterest, advertisers who use Promoted Pins received an average of 20 percent more (free) clicks in the month after the campaign[20].

Many of Pinterest's advertising options are suited to consumer goods rather than a large purchase such as a home, but understanding them is important to working with the site. For example, businesses can use Buyable Pins, which are a simple and secure way for buyers to purchase an item without leaving the site. They are identified by a blue "Buy It" price tag, which appears next to the red "Pin It" button on the top right corner of the screen.

Businesses can also employ Rich Pins. These add depth to four types of information: Product Pins give information on availability and pricing; App Pins allow for the download of an app directly from the site (currently available only in iOS); Article Pins show headline, author and story description; and Recipe Pins provide extra details such as ingredient lists, cooking times and serving sizes.

PINTEREST SCORECARD

- Do you have a strategy for your boards?

- Do your Pins link to your blog or website? Or somewhere else?

- Have you launched a rotating Showcase?

- Have you pinned your videos?

- Do you have more than 100 followers?

- Have you followed and interacted with anyone this week or month?

PINTEREST CHEAT SHEET

- Create a strategy for your boards based on what works for your business. If you are a remodeler, you might want to group pins by rooms and show before and after photos of bathrooms, kitchens, great rooms and more. If you don't start pinning with a plan in mind, your boards will become a mess like your teenagers room in no time.

- Your Pins must link back to your website or blog in order for Pinterest to send traffic to your website or blog. If you are linking somewhere else, you are just sending all of your potential traffic to them.

- Rotating Showcases run at the very top of Pinterest Pages and catch a lot of attention. Don't overlook this free billboard.

- Everyone loves videos and they watch them on all sorts of sites. Make sure to include yours on Pinterest as well.

- The more followers the better. People won't see your pins unless they are following you. Have a strategy to gain more followers, even if your strategy starts with following your own staff!

- If your pins and boards are quiet, maybe it is because you aren't reaching out to other Pinners. Make sure comment on other people's pins and save them as appropriate. In turn, they will do the same for you.

HOUZZ 11

When some couples traverse a stressful home remodeling project, they muddle through to completion, write it off as a life experience they hope not to repeat soon, and move on with life. Not Adi Tatarko and Alon Coehn. They used their experience to build Houzz, a social media platform aimed at easing the home improvement process on any scale, from decorating a room all the way to building a home from scratch. Since its introduction in 2009, Houzz has welcomed more than 40 million individuals and professionals from around the world.

From a user perspective, Houzz is a marketplace, a treasure map for discovery, a storehouse of ideas, and an access point to professional advice and services. Filled with 11 million images[1], which are organized into styles and categories, the site gives Houzzers the ability to place favorite photos and their own notes into Ideabooks. These can be made public, or they can be shared with specific Followers, who can offer feedback.

Users can start discussions among other users and ask questions of experts. They also have access to articles written and curated by Houzz's team of professional designers and writers.

For a home builder, Houzz is a showroom, a tool for collaborating with buyers, a professional networking group, and a direct connection to potential customers who are actively researching ways to improve their spaces. Yes, some are interested in a simple change of décor. With 40 million unique monthly visitors[2] checking things out, plenty who stop by are ready to remodel or build.

WHO USES HOUZZ?

- 40 million unique monthly visitors[3]

- 1.5 million trade professionals[4]

- 18,000 vendors with more than 8 million products[5]

- 74 percent of Houzzers plan to build, remodel or redecorate within two years[6].

- 90 percent of users are homeowners[7].

- 72 percent are between the ages of 25 and 54[8].

- Houzz users have an average household income of $125,000[9].

BASIC FEATURES AND TOOLS TO USE FOR BUSINESS

Register as a Pro. Builders and other industry professional can register with Houzz as a Pro to receive a free profile page, collaboration tools and a custom website. Include links to your blog, website and social media sites in your profile.

Upgrade to Pro+. For an additional cost, Pro+ members can place ads on the site and in the professionally written articles. They also enjoy enhanced placements and promotions within the site and can take advantage of analytics to gauge effectiveness and ROI.

Join the Houzz Trade Program. Receive trade-only pricing with discounts of up to 50 percent, free shipping on most orders over $49, and the ability to earn credits toward purchases[10] . You will also be able to pass on savings of 10 percent to your clients.

Take advantage of NAHB membership. Members of the National Association of Home Builders and local Home Builder Associations can qualify for discounts and special perks. Check with your HBA for more information.

Collaborate with Sketch. With Houzz's Sketch App, customers and professionals can use a photo from Houzz or their own photo to collaborate. Sketch offers the ability to write on the photo, circle features and add stickers for notes.

Share Ideabooks. Create Ideabooks of model homes, communities, landscaping, outdoor features or any specialties. Add notes to the images and to the Ideabook descriptions using key search terms.

Respond to discussion questions. Professionals can bookmark and follow topics in their areas of expertise and join discussions when appropriate. Participating in discussions raises visibility on the site, establishes expertise and demonstrates good customer service/attentiveness.

Submit projects for editorial features. Follow the instructions on the site to submit Ideabooks and other projects for editorial features. Houzz's writers and editors highlight projects and topics based on merit rather than paid sponsorships.

Solicit customer reviews. The "Get Reviews" feature allows professionals to email customers or industry partners from within the site, providing a direct link where they can leave a review. The Houzz widget can be placed on the corporate website to provide a direct link to add reviews, too. Professionals with a greater number of reviews rank higher for site searches in specific geographic areas.

ADVERTISING

To advertise on Houzz, you must have a Houzz Pro+ account. This gives your company an enhanced directory placement as well as ads in the photo stream, in advice, and in the stories section. Other benefits are being promoted in the newsletter, inbound call tracking, analytics and a pro spotlight sponsored article. The price of advertising is not disclosed on the site and most likely varies by market, so contact Houzz to get a quote.

HOUZZ SCORECARD

- Have you completed your professional profile, including key search terms for your geographic area as well as your offerings?

- Have you included links to your blog and your website in your profile, project descriptions and Ideabooks?

- Are you active in the discussion and advice forums?

- Have you added a Houzz Badge or widget (to allow reviews or provide a slide-show of a project) to your website?

- Have you created Ideabooks?

- Have you submitted projects or Ideabooks for editorial features?

HOUZZ CHEAT SHEET

- Completing your professional profile with key search terms for your geographic area will help you to be found more often.

- Including links to your blog and your website in your profile, project descriptions, and Ideabooks will send traffic from Houzz back to your website.

- Participating in the discussion and advice forums could engage you with future clients.

- Displaying the Houzz Badge or widget on your website not only makes reviews easy to give and provides a project slideshow, but offering these will boost your ranking in Houzz directories.

- Your Ideabooks will help Houzzers to get ideas, and if they like enough of your Ideabooks, they might just hire you to build their next house or complete that remodel.

- Getting your projects or Ideabooks submitted for editorial features means you are in the running for lots of free publicity on the site. Show off that great project that you just finished.

INSTAGRAM 12

I ntroduced in 2010 and purchased by Facebook in 2012, Instagram focuses on using visuals to tell a story. With 800 million active users and 500 million[1] of them using the site every day. Instagram is the second most popular social media platform[2]. In July 2017, 15 million business used Instagram, compared with 8 million just four months earlier[3]. According to Instagram's blog, the majority of these are small- and medium-sized businesses[4].

Why are businesses flocking to the platform? Eighty percent of those millions of active users follow at least one business[5], which tells us that users are open to and perhaps even expect to engage with businesses that interest them. The app's simple, uncluttered design makes it easier for businesses to get noticed. In a Facebook-sponsored biometrics study that compared engagement among identical ads on Instagram, Twitter, Pinterest, and Facebook, participants paid most attention to those displayed on Instagram. Participants also displayed a slightly higher physiological response to Instagram ads and overall feeds, indicating a deeper engagement with the platform than with the other social media channels. Of the amount of time participants spent on display ads, they were much more focused on the image than on any accompanying words[6].

WHO USES INSTAGRAM?

Let's take a look at some Instagram statistics[7]:

- 700 million active users

- 40 billion photos had been shared as of January 2017.

- 4.2 billion posts are liked each day.

- 95 million photos are uploaded per day as of January 2017, compared to 70 million per day in 2016.

- 68 percent of users are female.

- 77.6 million active users live in the U.S.

- 32 percent of all internet users are on the platform. Broken down further, this includes 59 percent of users aged 18–29 and 33 percent of users aged 30–49. 38 percent of female internet users and 26 percent of male users have Instagram accounts.

Instagram is a photo sharing and video sharing app that works from your smartphone. Individuals and companies upload photos or videos and then add various filters to enhance their images. The location of the image can be added with a geotag. And, adding a hashtag means that others with similar interests might search and find your post. Posts can be shared from a user's Instagram account to their other social media profiles.

BASIC FEATURES AND TOOLS FOR BUSINESS

Now that Instagram has profiles for individuals and for businesses, make sure that you have a business profile. The benefit to a business profile is that you can add a phone number to your bio. And, you get access to analytics that you don't have access to as an individual. The only clickable link that Instagram provides is in the bio section under your name. Most companies never change this, but a strategy that I've noticed recently is to use this as a link to register for an event or a VIP list or whatever big news that the business wants to share. My biggest pet peeve of Instagram is that the site is a trap that wants you to stay on it. I'd love to see clickable links included in posts so that users could get more information on the post from the company's website.

Stories

One of the newest Instagram features is Stories. This popular feature allows users add photos and video to a story. It doesn't matter how many photos and videos are added to tell your Story. They will play in the sequence they were added.

Instagram reports that 250 million daily active users utilize stories and that they have greatly increased time on site[8]. The content added to Stories disappears after 24 hours, unless you save the Story to your device (smartphone or tablet) to reuse in the future.

Live video was added to Stories functionality in November 2016. Other updates to Stories include augmented reality stickers and face filters. Individuals aren't the only ones embracing Stories, more than half of the businesses on the site posted a Story during July 2017. Even more impressive, Instagram reports that one in five Stories shared resulted in the business receiving a direct message on the app.

Stories are only available on the mobile app, but it is possible to send Instagram Stories as a direct message (DM). This is the perfect way to send a short video to prospects or the homeowner who is out of town while you are remodeling their house.

There are a number of benefits to using Stories as part of your social media plan:

- Prominent placement—Stories are seen at the top of the app in a prominent, "can't miss" position.

- The bar for the quality of these photos and videos isn't set as high because most of these images are captured on the fly.

- Collaboration with other users is possible by tagging them in the post, for example @CarolMorgan007

- Face filters, text and stickers allow for easy editing.

- Experimentation is fun. Try different content types: photo, short video, Boomerang, Rewind and live video and see which your audience embraces.

- Users can search Stories for hashtags and locations to see what is going on in subject matter that they are interested in, or just what is happening nearby.

Stories now offer users the ability to Go Live and share video with followers in real time. When the video ends, it is no longer available for viewing unless you share a

to your story in the future. To save your video for the future, when you are
ng, tap "end" in the top right then tap to confirm. Then, tap "save" in the
save it to your camera roll or share it to your Story.

Videos

Instagram posts with videos get twice the engagement on the platform than photos, plus they enjoy a higher rate of shares to other platforms[9]. Videos can be recorded and shared from within the app (this is best for in-the-moment videos without much editing) or from other sources. Videos can be from 3 to 60 seconds and, unlike in the apps early days of video, sound is included.

Hashtags

Hashtags can expand your companies reach on Instagram. (See our earlier hashtag coverage in Chapter 5 Mobile, Visuals, and Hashtags: Social Media Must-Haves) The hashtags you use can be general or specific to a campaign, just make sure they are relevant and not spammy. Set up a hashtag for your company #yourbrandname (#denimmarketing). Most companies use three to five hashtags, but every now and then you see a post with up to 30 hashtags. Using hashtags makes your content more discoverable.

With authentic posts, users will be more likely to comment on and like the posts. This is where companies should respond, create conversation and build relationships.

According to HashTags.com[10], the popular hashtags for home builders include:

#moving	#home	#texas
#realestate	#homesweethome	#adhouseplans
#newhomes	#living	#architecturaldesigns
#quickmovein	#homebuilder	#houseplan
#dreamhome	#southwestern	#architecture
#inspiration	#stucco	#architect
#instahome	#sanantonio	#newhome

#newconstruction   #dreamhouse   #luxuryhome

#newhouse   #homeplan   #JustListed

#homedesign   #architectural

#homeconstruction   #craftsman

Brand Your Content

Find creative ways to convey the look and feel of your brand through imagery. Many companies add their logo to all of their images, but there are companies that have perfected showing their brand without a logo. Some tips include choosing a color palate and always using the same filter.

Raving Fans

I love it when fans do the heavy lifting for a business. Ask your loyal followers to post photos using a hashtag that is specific to your company and then repost these to Instagram or even Facebook. Because people love to see themselves and their pictures on social media, they will like and comment on these. Make sure to use the @ symbol to tag them in the images and alert them. Using fans to promote your company adds a layer of authenticity to your posts and page.

Promote Open Houses and Events

Use Instagram to spread the word on your events and open houses. Promote the upcoming BBQ for current homeowners and prospects, your newly remodeled Parade of Homes entry, that next Grand Opening, etc. Along with images or videos of the home or community, include the date, time, and location as well as relevant hashtags.

Topics

Creating buckets of content has become a popular way to plan for upcoming content. Consider adding Model Home Monday, This or That, Throwback Thursday, Floorplan Friday, or a myriad of other topics to your content plan.

Filters—Use Them!

Instagram has a plethora of filters that can be used to enhance images. Since you don't always have a professional photographer with you, filters provide an easy way to adjust the brightness and the contrast of a smartphone image. Of course, they have all the fun face filters too so that selfies or just regular pictures can be a little more fun.

Host a Contest

A quick way to garner new fans on Instagram is to host a contest. Invite followers to enter your contest by taking a picture and tagging it with the campaign hashtag. Also invite them to follow the corporate Instagram. Host a random drawing from among the participants and give them a prize such as a gift card or a basket of goodies.

ADVERTISING

Instagram ads launched in 2013 and have become an easy way to brand lift and recall. Promoted posts can be set up through the Instagram app directly. And, more robust ad campaigns can be set up through Facebook's Ad Manager or Power Editor. Instagram offers three ad formats—photo ads, video ads or carousel ads featuring multiple images. Ads can have a variety of goals, including increasing awareness of a brand, driving traffic to a company's website, increasing sales, raising post engagement and more. Ads can be targeted by location, demographics, interests, behaviors, custom audiences, lookalike audiences or with automatic targeting.

INSTAGRAM SCORECARD

- Do you post once a week?

- Are you following everyone that follows you?

- Do your posts include hashtags?

- Have you hosted an Instagram contest in the last year?

INSTAGRAM CHEAT SHEET

- The more frequently you post, the more often your company will be seen.

- Make sure that you look at your followers and follow the ones that are appropriate. Also look at who your competitors follow and who follows them.

- Using hashtags in your posts greatly expands the reach of each post.

- Instagram contests are one of the best ways to expand your list of followers.

SNAPCHAT 13

I n the world of social media, Snapchat takes on the role of the sleeping giant, lying quiet while slowly taking over the incoming social media influencers: millennials and Generation Z. In the last year there has even been a noticeable growth in users over 35.

Snapchat is a social media platform introduced in 2011 by former Stanford students Bobby Murphy, Reggie Brown, and CEO Evan Spiegel. The app allows users to send seconds-long videos and images directly to their Snap friends and/or share with their followers via Snap stories that can be viewed for a user-specified length of time before they become inaccessible.

WHO USES SNAPCHAT?

- Snapchat has 173 million daily users[1].

- Daily active users open the app an average of 18 times a day[2].

- Users spend, on average, 25–30 minutes a day on Snapchat[3].

- 77 percent of social media-using college students use Snapchat at least once a day[4].

- 45 percent of college students would open a Snapchat from a brand they don't know[5].

- 73 percent of college students would open a Snapchat from a brand they do know[6].

- 58 percent of college students would be most likely to purchase a brand's product or service if they were sent a coupon on Snapchat[7].

BASIC FEATURES AND TOOLS TO USE FOR BUSINESS

The Snapchat vernacular can be confusing. When users open Snapchat, their screen automatically opens to the camera. Users take either a front- or back-facing photo or video, with or without an interactive lens, and have the option to send their "snap" directly to an individual(s) and/or to post it to their Snap story. Previously, Snapchat only allowed photos to be visible to viewers for up to 10 seconds, but users now have the option for the photo to be viewable for infinity, or as long as the receiver chooses to view it, and videos can either loop or play only once, whereas in the past it only showed the one time. Filters and text can be overlaid on the photo or video before sending for additional effect. Viewers have the option to screenshot snaps, but the sender will be notified.

Snap stories are only available for 24 hours, but can be downloaded and shared on other social media platforms. Users can also contribute snaps to local news stories for user generated news. This allows viewers to see events and news from different angles and perspectives.

Some of the most popular ways that businesses use Snapchat are with behind-the-scenes sneak peeks, Q&As, incentives, and giveaways. Whether millennials are currently your target market or not, they eventually will be, so it is important to know exactly how to reach them when the time is right. Alternatively, millennials do not respond to advertising the way that past generations do. They practice a higher sense of product loyalty, particularly with businesses that contribute to the local community and do not blatantly "advertise" to them. Millennials appreciate and respond to brands that put forth an effort to care about them as people, something that does not just happen overnight, but is developed over time. To which I say "there is no better time than the present" to acknowledge and get to know your millennial audience. Case in point, you need to care about Snapchat.

A potential drawback to managing Snapchat business, users can only be signed into one profile at a time, with no capability to switch between profiles. Users must log in and out between profiles, and there is no scheduling option for snaps. Snaps must be live-captured within the app or manually uploaded from the Memories function.

Additionally, there is no real way to track the number of followers a company or person has on Snapchat. The closest numbers would come from monitoring the number of Snap story views right before the story expires. But even that is flawed because what if a handful of followers were not in a position to check Snapchat in that 24 hours? Even still, monitoring the number of story views is the best guess.

ADVERTISING

Snapchat offers three advertising avenues for companies: Snap Ads, Filters, and Lenses. Snap Ads have the option to either be video (motion graphic, live, cinemagraph, or GIF-style) or still.

Geofilters can be purchased for promoting an event, business, or specific location and serve as an excellent way to get a company's branding on photos to further drive awareness, promotion, and a Call to Action all in one device. Anyone can create their own filter within the app and set geometric parameters, also known as a geofence, for its use.

Lenses on Snapchat are the most interactive way for businesses to interact with their customers. Whether it is promoting a holiday that connects to your business or a time of year, lenses are the ultimate, creative tool on Snapchat. Visit https://forbusiness.snapchat.com/gettingstarted/ to learn more about advertising with Snapchat.

Snapchat Discover is the corporate advertising platform within the app, allowing users to view content generated by outstanding media. Discover stories link to articles and graphics and utilize both video and photo. The most popular Snapchat Discover stories are BuzzFeed, Comedy Central, Food Network and ESPN—which is really no surprise as the platform is most prominently utilized by millennials.

To be clear, Snapchat Discover is not typically used by small businesses. To get the most out of Snapchat for small business, utilize the tool yourself and become a Snapchat superstar by posting daily story posts that drive engagement such as "Screenshot this snap to receive $100 off your next service!" Share posts with your username and Snapcode on your other social media channels that drive viewers and followers to your business' Snapchat. For example, "Follow us on Snapchat to receive instant savings before today's story expires!"

Snapchat provides users with their own unique Snapcode which utilizes the platform's ghost image and QR coding. Users can either take a selfie within the ghost frame, or edit the Snapcode to include their logo. But be careful not to edit anything outside of the ghost frame or your Snapcode will not work and users will not be able to follow you with it.

Take a look at the below tips and tricks to learn how to kick off your business' Snapchat superstardom.

- **Update content.** Snap stories should be updated frequently, if not daily. Updates can include anything as simple as day-to-day operations to show what it is like to work at your company. Behind-the-scenes looks are enough to generate a true following and serve as additional content to post on other social sites to gain new followers in real time and after the fact when you upload the story as a video to Facebook as evidence that "We are active on Snapchat, be sure to follow us so you don't miss our updates!"

- **Interaction is key.** Followers, in particular millennials, like to know that a company and brand is real and that they care enough about their consumers to interact with them. Add back new followers, and be sure to respond to any messages within the chat app or direct photo snaps!

- **Utilize Snapchat ads**. Sponsor a Snap ad or lens to drive engagement and awareness, or create a custom geofilter. Geofilters are the most economical option for small businesses.

- **Document memorable moments.** Use Snapchat to share and save memorable moments such as awards, birthdays, new employees and more.

- **Host a takeover.** Whether it is a popular social media personality, which usually comes at a cost, or an employee, publicize them taking over the company Snapchat for the day on other channels to drive new followers.

Still not convinced that Snapchat is a worthy tool for your business? Facebook certainly thinks it is a business worthy platform and sees the video and image-messaging tool as a threat to its reign over social media. Why else would Facebook continue to release Instagram updates (the conglomerate purchased Instagram in 2012 for $1 billion) that oddly enough resemble attributes known to Snapchat, such as stories, text overlay, stickers, etc.

Snapchat has served as a breakout app for video, photo and text messaging. Nearly every update provides an innovative addition to the platform. In 2017 alone, Snapchat users have been introduced to Snap Map, group-specified Snapchat stories, limitless snap time, looped videos, and let's not forget Snapchat Spectacles. For the latest Snapchat updates, visit www.Snap.com/en-US/news.

SNAPCHAT SCORECARD

- Are snaps are made regularly if not daily?

- Is the content is engaging and informational?

- Does the profile communicate with others via messages and snapped photos?

- Does the Snapcode include the company logo and colors?

SNAPCHAT CHEAT SHEET

- Engagement is key. If you are going to use Snapchat, then use it frequently.

- Images don't have to be professional. Use lenses and filters to spice up your content. A "boring day at the office" can look surprisingly exciting on Snapchat thanks to these tools.

- Set up a Snapchat geofilter for your next networking/business event and promote its availability on the company Story and other social media channels.

- Set up a branded Snapcode for your business. It will help you to attract more followers.

YOUTUBE 14

As we discussed in Chapter 5 Mobile, Visuals, and Hashtags: Social Media Must-Haves, video is an integral part of any digital marketing plan. Video can capture attention, fuel imagination, tell a business's story clearly, and display products in the format potential home buyers want to see them.

And of the social media platforms, which was the first to become a widely used video sharing site? YouTube, of course!

Founded in 2005 by three former PayPal employees and purchased by Google in 2006, YouTube is often called the world's second largest search engine. The platform boasts 1.3 billion users who upload 300 hours of video each minute and watch almost 5 billion videos per day[1].

In an overall marketing plan, YouTube is useful as both a standalone social media platform and as a complement to other marketing. For example, since YouTube, Google search, and Google+ are siblings of the same parent company, the work put into a YouTube presence flows directly into a Google+ profile and has the potential to improve search rankings. Plus, each uploaded video has an embed code that can be used on a website or blog.

In establishing a YouTube presence, businesses will create an account. The process is most efficient for businesses already on Google+ because a link from the Google+ profile will create a YouTube account, bringing over information and images. If the YouTube account is created first, a linked Google+ account is automatically created.

A YouTube account can have multiple channels to highlight different niches. In the case of a homebuilder, different channels can highlight various new home communities, home styles or floor plans. Instead of friends or followers, YouTube channels have subscribers, who receive notifications of new uploads. Anyone can watch a video on YouTube. Registered users can comment on, rate and share content as well.

WHO USES YOUTUBE?

- 1.3 billion people[2]

- YouTube is accessible to 95 percent of all Internet users[3]

- 900 million unique visits per month[4]

- One billion mobile video views per day[5]

- The length of an average session on a mobile device is 40 minutes[6].

- In an average month, eight out of 10 adults ages 18–49 watch a YouTube video[7].

- 50 percent of users are male, 50 percent female, though men make up most viewers in 90 percent of the content categories[8].

- 70 percent of users are watching YouTube from mobile devices[9].

- More 18–49-year-old viewers than any cable network (and that's just on mobile)[10].

- Time spent on YouTube by adults over 35 is growing 40 percent faster than overall growth. Time spent by just the over 55 group is growing 80 percent faster than overall growth[11].

- 62 percent of Millennials say they are likely to act after viewing a YouTube ad, while 51 percent of viewers ages 35 and older say the same[12].

- Millennials prefer YouTube more than two times more than television[13].

BASIC FEATURES AND TOOLS
TO USE FOR BUSINESS

Video hosting platform. YouTube provides embedded codes so uploaded videos can be placed directly on websites, blogs or other social media platforms. Unique URLs from YouTube can be inserted into email marketing. *Note:* YouTube videos embedded on Facebook will not automatically start running or feature a preview as videos that are native to Facebook will.

Cards. From the Video Manager view, it's easy to add up to five cards to a video. These informational boxes can be used to direct viewers to another video, playlist, or channel; to highlight a nonprofit organization; to poll viewers; or to provide links to your website or other associated sites. Cards should be relevant to the video content and those that could encourage viewers to jump to something else should be placed toward the end of the video.

Activity sharing. Set your account to inform other social platforms when you upload, comment on or share a video.

First-comment pin. Control the first comment that appears under a video by pinning it. This can be changed as more comments are received.

Subtitles. Subtitles are useful not only for the hearing impaired, but also for viewers who do not want to watch a video with sound. They're easy to add with auto captioning and a little editing for accuracy.

Custom subscribe button. Invite viewers to subscribe to a channel by uploading an image to be displayed in all videos. Customize the image and the timing of its placement within videos.

Opportunities for search optimization. Account profile, channel descriptions, individual video descriptions, and categories/tags all offer opportunities to employ keywords and maximize visibility in a search.

360-degree video and 3D video. YouTube allows the upload of these videos, which are hugely popular with homebuyers.

Live streaming. Live streaming is available in several different contexts, including versions that allow for streaming from mobile or webcam, previews and backup redundancy. To live stream from a mobile device, a channel must have at least 100 subscribers.

ADVERTISING

YouTube offers many formats for advertising, including display ads that appear next to a video, overlay ads that appear in the lower 20 percent of the video, sponsored cards, and skippable and nonskippable video. The YouTube Director App offers takes a user through a series of steps and offers to help business create their own quality video ads easily and quickly.

YOUTUBE SCORECARD

- Do your profile and channels match the branding on other sites and platforms?

- Do all videos include CTAs either within the video or within the text?

- Do you communicate with viewers and other users?

- Is each video optimized with keywords, categories, and tags?

- Are YouTube videos shared across social media channels?

- Is there a variety of content and are there multiple channels?

YOUTUBE CHEAT SHEET

- Use consistent images, colors and messaging so the YouTube account matches the corporate website, blog, and other social media platforms.

- Calls to Action could include asking viewers to share, comment or visit the company blog or website

- Interactivity involves monitoring and responding to comments on your own videos and also commenting on and sharing videos of others, possibly including vendors, real estate agents, industry groups or other partners. Comments should add value by specifically referencing something in the video or asking a question to start a discussion. Comments include a link to the commenter's channel, but hyperlinks cannot be manually added to a comment.

- Make sure to add appropriate keywords and descriptions so that when viewers search on YouTube they find you.

- Create account settings that allow Activity Sharing. New uploads, comments and shares will appear in other social media accounts as specified.

- Ideas for content and channels include corporate (history, team member specialties, nonprofit support), new home communities, design elements, home styles, and floor plans.

OTHER DIGITAL MARKETING 15

N ow that we have taken a fairly deep dive into the various social media sites, let's look at some other digital marketing tactics that are effective in reaching various audiences. Because marketing isn't one size fits all (and for that matter, neither are clothes), it is nice to have a variety of tactics to choose from. After all, you might not be comfortable on video, but might find that you love hosting a podcast.

PODCASTS

Think of podcasts as Talk Radio but on the internet. Much like setting up your iTunes or Spotify account to listen to music, you can set up your smartphone or other device to download your favorite podcast shows so that you can listen to episodes as you have time—on your morning jog, during your commute, in between meetings, etc.

Podcasts are series of audio files available on demand. These show series can be played by your smartphone through a variety of podcast tools such as Apple Podcasts, Google Play Music, Spotify or Pocket Casts.

The variety and abundance of shows and subjects can be overwhelming. There is something for everyone on podcasts from politics to self-help to real estate shows.

Podcasting also has business benefits. It is a great way to create content for the company's website and social media. Not everyone is comfortable with writing blogs or being on video, so podcasting offers an alternative way to create content.

According to Edison Research[1], 67 million Americans listen to podcasts each month and the trend is growing because of the smartphone.

If you think producing a podcast is a tool that would benefit your business, spend some time reviewing and setting goals. Is the goal of your show content generation, showcasing expertise, business development, or increasing traffic?

Content generation is time consuming and something many companies struggle with. Creating quality content that is original is difficult for many. However, being interviewed can make it a lot easier on people who would rather just talk that write. A half or full day recording session can easily return six to eight podcasts (after editing) and the bulk of a company's blog posts for a month. The quality of your guests will determine the quality of your content. Make sure to invest time in guest recruitment.

Showcasing expertise on your unique selling point or a specific facet of the industry is important to gain credibility with potential buyers and trade partners. Create a show around energy efficiency, green building, selling to the 55 plus buyer, financing or even create ways to get millennials into their first home.

Business development can be a primary or secondary goal of your podcast. Having a public forum to promote vendors and industry partners can help to develop deeper business relationships. Inviting people to be interviewed on your show is a great way to meet and connect with people who are potentially important to your business.

Increased traffic and reaching new audiences is pretty much a given for a podcast. Your show will provide great interactive information for your existing platform, but more than that it becomes a way to syndicate content that will in turn attract new audiences. Because people consume content differently, it is important to provide them with a variety of choices—some watch videos, some read, others watch TV and then there are those who like to listen to audio. Think of your podcast as an additional layer of content, just like a video or a 3D tour. You want to reach your audience where they are with their preferred format, no matter what that is.

I started Atlanta Real Estate Forum Radio as a podcast in October of 2011 with Intrepid Studio, LLC and my friend and co-host Todd Schnick. The show has proven to be a great outreach tool in the Atlanta real estate market and has helped us promote our blog to new readers, as well as reach an entirely new audience of iTunes listeners.

Todd adds, "Podcasting is a great way to create content, reach new audiences and syndicate your messages to new audiences. Make sure to think about these four things when launching an online show: goals, content (guest recruitment), distribution, and production." We've talked about goals and content earlier in this section, so let's dive into distribution and production.

How will your podcast get distributed? Will you use the popular iOS or Google podcast apps? Then, how will you syndicate the show? I'd suggest looking at all of your social media channels, email marketing as well as public relations.

Producing a podcast is relatively inexpensive because of the number of free tools, apps, and open-source platforms available on the internet. You can record your audio by using the voice recorder apps that come with most phones, or by downloading an app called SoundCloud. You can then edit your audio podcasts using GarageBand (on Apple), or with a free download called Audacity (where Atlanta Real Estate Forum Radio is edited). You can publish direct to iTunes (for free), or to Stitcher. With the right tools, producing and publishing audio content has never been simpler or less expensive.

BLOGGING

I mentioned earlier in the book about the importance of content and blogging. Don't take my word for it; let's review some statistics from HubSpot[2].

- 53 percent of marketers say blog content creation is their top inbound marketing priority.

- One in 10 blog posts are compounding, meaning organic search increases their traffic over time.

- Compounding blog posts make up 10% of all blog posts and generate 38% of overall traffic.

- Over its lifetime, one compounding blog post creates as much traffic as six decaying posts.

- Companies that published 16 or more blog posts per month got almost three and a half times more traffic than companies that published four or fewer monthly posts.

- Business-to-business companies that blogged 11 or more times per month had almost three times more traffic than those blogging just once per month, or not at all.

- Business-to-consumer companies that blogged 11 or more times per month got more than four times as many leads than those that blog only four or five times per month.

- Companies that published 16 or more blog posts per month got about four and a half times more leads than companies that published four or fewer monthly posts.

Still not sold on blogging? Search Engine Journal[3] says, "blogging is critical in 2017."

Including a blog (or news section built as a blog) in your website is clearly a way to differentiate your website and company from competitors. The reason that blogging works is that even though all blog posts display on a single page together, the search engines see each one as a new independent page on your website. Each blog post has its own unique content, keyword, and data for search engine optimization. So, every time you post a new blog, you alert the search engines and tell them to come back to look at your website to see what is new and index it. This helps increase traffic to your blog/website.

Of course, search engine optimization is just one reason to blog, another great reason is to create a platform to engage with buyers…one that you own and control. Great content will help keep current customers engaged, while converting new customers by providing them with the information they need to make a decision. Your blog differentiates your company from the competition with increasing interest tin your products and services.

Blogging makes all of that content for social media easier! Once you have written a blog post, you can syndicate the content from your blog to all of your social media pages. This provides your social sites with much needed content, while at the same time providing a link back to your website/blog from every article on social.

Most web developers will happily add a WordPress blog to your website in a folder. Some things to consider as you launch your new blog:

1 · What Plugins do you need?

- **Yoast.** This tool makes search engine optimization easy with its built in self-check tool.

- **Askimet.** This is the ultimate spam catcher

- **Sociable.** This plug-in allows your readers to share your site's posts to their social media accounts—Facebook, Twitter, Pinterest, etc.

- **MailChimp for WordPress.** This adds the ability to sign up for your newsletter seamlessly from your blog.

- **Breadcrumb NavXT.** This shows website visitors where they have been.

You can also use plug-ins to add a calendar, a countdown timer for a big event, and many more features. You install and activate plug-ins from the WordPress dashboard. Visit WordPress (www.wordpress.org/extend/plugins/) to browse more than 50,000 plug-ins. If you have ever thought, "I wish my blog could… " it probably can. Try not to get carried away; installing too many gadgets will distract users and make your blog slow to load and respond. Just focus on the basic plug-ins necessary to control spam comments, generate site maps, and enhance SEO.

2 · **Create a content calendar.** Having a schedule for the content that is running on the blog makes it easier for all team members. The content on the blog should tie into the overall marketing plan and be included in your social media content plan.

3 · **Set up categories.** Begin with a plan for how to organize your posts, whether by community or city, trends, news, etc. Think this through before you start posting, and please rename the uncategorized category "News" or something that makes sense. For true bloggers and WordPress developers, seeing uncategorized is like nails on a chalkboard.

4 · **Determine keywords.** Work with your internal or external SEO resource and determine what keywords you want to use in your posts. As you are writing, be aware of how your posts come across to the reader. You want your posts to read naturally and not stuff keywords into them just for the sake of making sure they are there. Consider using synonyms and phrases, not just individual words.

5 · **Track effectiveness.** Make sure that your website team installs Google Analytics or another tracking software to ensure you know what works and what needs improvement on the site. Track key performance indicators such as number of visitors, time on site, and most popular content. Google allows you to track visitors on your site that come from the social networks. It is interesting to see which ones convert and where they spend time.

What makes a good blog post?

First of all, it should be interesting for the person reading it! It also needs to have content that the search engines see as original. It goes without saying that it contains stunning visuals—photos, video, graphics or an infographic. And, when it was posted, SEO was a consideration, not an afterthought.

Blog posts need to be between 350–1,400 words. If your plan is to post eight posts a month, vary the length and have a goal of one to two really long comprehensive posts, one or two shorter posts (maybe describe an image or a video), and then three or four posts in the 300–500 word range.

Tips for creating great blog content:

- Write an attention-grabbing headline. So much content is produced on a daily basis that it's important to make yours stand out. The headline is also a great way to incorporate keywords and ensure the site ranks well for the right search terms.

- Get to the point. It's a busy world we live in, so don't include lots of extra "fluff" that your audience isn't interested in reading. Just say what you need to say.

- Don't be afraid to write a super long blog post with valuable information. We all read a lot of content online and we want to read well-written, informative posts. People will tune in and read an 800- to 1,500-word blog if it's interesting and provides information they need or want.

- Break up long content and keep it interesting by incorporating lists, bullets, numbers, infographics and images. Top 3 lists, Top 5 lists, and bulleted information attract attention. This makes it easier for readers to absorb the information and understand what action to take.

- Don't hide your personality online when you're writing. Posts should be conversational and interesting. Consider writing your blog posts in first person instead of third person marketing speak. Readers are trying to make a personal connection with a brand or company, and the blog is one of the best ways to allow that connection to happen.

- Make sure your content is new and written in an original way. No one wants to spend 15 minutes reading old information that's being regurgitated from somewhere else.

- The most effective posts will provide information most buyers are seeking, so describe your community's location, homes, and amenities. Readers may also want to know how to obtain financing or receive tax and energy credits.

- Have a Call to Action in your blog pointing your audience in the next direction. Is your blog about a new home? Then tell them how to find out more information about that home or how to get to it. Are you writing about an upcoming event? Then make sure you provide links for purchasing tickets or getting directions.

Finally, the last step in creating a successful blog is making sure that content can be shared easily. Your content can't go viral if your readers can't share it! Most blog platforms provide social media widgets or apps that make sharing a breeze. You can even incorporate special call-outs within your blog highlighting important quotes or points that will turn them directly into a tweet. Treat your blog like the content-producing and syndication machine it is, and share every post to your social media site. Plug-ins can be added to WordPress sites to make some of the syndication automatic, but often the best results are achieved by posting natively to each individual site.

Some things to think about when you want engagement from readers:

- What is the action you want your readers to take? (Think comments, social shares, clicks, subscribes, and even sales)

- How have you inspired them to take action in the past?

- How does your content contribute to successful interactions? (Is your content provocative, visionary, relevant, current, and timely?)

Promote Your Blog

Burn the real simple syndication (RSS) feed, and use it to set up a recurring email of your most recent blog post to your subscribers. Register the blog on blog catalogs such as Technorati, Blog Catalog, and Best of the Web. Make sure to promote your news site or blog from your social sites, your website, and in your email signature. Your blog is a core component of your online marketing strategy. It serves to keep your website updated with fresh, engaging, and optimized content to rank well in Google's search results.

EMAIL MARKETING

Email marketing is still a very useful and important marketing strategy. Yes, people actually still read emails! According to MailChimp[4] statistics most email marketing campaigns have an open rate of 20 percent or better. And, Statista[5] shows that campaigns with a personal message have a better open rate than those without a personal message.

There are actually three different types of email marketing campaigns that you should consider utilizing:

1 · **Welcome email.** When a form on your website is completed, the prospect, client or partner should receive a welcome email. This email should be automatically generated by whatever email marketing program you use. It should thank the prospect for contacting you, send them any information that was promised to them and inform them that someone will follow up directly by email of phone with them. Don't make this correspondence too complicated as they are really just looking for the information that caused them to contact you

2 · **Recurring emails or automatically-generated emails.** Set up a series of emails to send to prospects after they have received your welcome email. Choose the frequency of how often prospects will receive these emails and create a series of 10 or more messages. The messages should feature evergreen content. In other words, content that is not going to need to be updated frequently or feature specific promotions. Some topics that work well: thank you, our team, our philosophy, awards, move into your dream home (with a link to quick-delivery homes so they can see current inventory), buyer incentives, preferred lenders, credit repair classes, happy homeowner testimonials, online chat, construction process, remodeling process, rent versus buy, green building, energy efficiency, should I remodel?, warranty, connect with us on social, etc. The number of topics is really limitless, and your business practices and unique selling proposition will help you to come up with ideas for topics. The frequency of how often you send these can vary. MarketingSherpa[6] reports that 61 percent of people are fine receiving a monthly promotional email. You will find a lot of different studies and opinions on how often you should send email, but every two or three weeks seems to work well.

3 · Promotional emails. These emails feature a promotion, incentive, event or new product or plan. Consider announcing your July 4th promotion, inventory reduction sale, latest Realtor promotion, new floor plan, grand opening of a new community, amenity opening, new hire, before and after of that latest remodel, etc. Because promotional emails are topical, they should be sent as you have news. The best emails have a targeted CTA, so invite them to an event or give them a clear Call to Action. Use limited offers or limited time frames to hook your prospect with a valuable offer that speaks genuinely about your brand.

Newsletter or Magazine

Creating a monthly newsletter or magazine can be a great way to keep prospects engaged. One easy way to do this is to create a template that pulls specific blog posts into it. You can schedule it to go out once a month and always pull the blogs that are in the newsletter category.

Some tips for creating a great newsletter:

- **Determine the subject for your newsletter**—product news, new communities, new agents, news coverage, etc. Have a common theme so that it isn't a random mess.

- **Use a super clean design.** Give your reader's eyes a break from all of the clutter on the internet and in their inbox. Think minimal text and minimal images with lots of white space.

- **Make it educational.** Give them a reason to read it. Instead of telling them that you are great at email marketing, consider telling them how to do their own email marketing and give them tips. Striking a balance between education and promotion will serve you well. Strive to educate, not just promote your products. So for a homebuilder, this might mean that you educate them on the benefits of buying a new home, or using a certified green builder. Incorporate design trends, ways to declutter, how to live in your home and still have it look like a model home.

- **Make your subject lines fun and creative.** There is no guarantee that they will read your email even if it makes it past your spam filter.

- **Have a Call to Action.** Everything you do should have a CTA. Yes; even the monthly newsletter. What is the one thing you want them to do when they read it? Make that the focus whether it is clicking to read the full blog post, registering for a VIP list or sharing the newsletter with a friend.

- **Opt in / opt out.** Make it super easy to opt into your newsletter and to opt out when they are ready to leave. Nothing makes me madder than scrolling to the bottom of an email and finding no way to escape from it showing up in my email box time and time again.

- **Measure twice, cut once.** Once you have added content to your newsletter, make sure to test it. Send it to an internal review team to review it for broken links, wrong dates, typos, etc. Only after they sign off on it should you hit send and distribute it to the masses.

- **Co-marketing or co-branded email.** Consider partnering on email marketing with your preferred lender, siding company, termite company, or other partner. There is certainly value in telling your prospects about your strong industry relationships and the quality products and services that you are delivering to them.

CAN-SPAM Act

When you set up your email marketing program, you need to use an email blasting software that will help your company stay compliant with the CAN-SPAM Act. The CAN-SPAM Act covers a lot more than just bulk email. It covers all commercial messages, which the law defines as "any electronic mail message the primary purpose of which is the commercial advertisement or promotion of a commercial product or service," including email that promotes content on commercial websites. There is no exception for business-to-business email. That means all email (e.g., a message to former customers announcing a new product line) must comply with the law.

If you email anyone on behalf of a business, the laws apply. The CAN-SPAM Act creates rules for commercial email and messages and gives recipients the right to stop receiving your emails. And, there are penalties of up to $40,654 for companies that violate the rules.

Programs like MailChimp (www.mailchimp.com), Constant Contact (www.constant-contact.com), or iContact (www.icontact.com) provide templates and guidance on how to not get labeled as a spammer or reported to the Federal Trade Commission. These programs also will allow you to send HTML emails and newsletters that are easily read on any number of devices. They also have super savvy tracking built into them, so you can easily view opens and clicks per each individual campaign. This will help you determine who is interested in what aspect of your businesses and how to follow up with them next. Make sure that you have included your social media links in your emails as well. Make it easy for readers to like your content and to follow your pages.

You are liable for your email messages even if you have hired another company or person to send email on your behalf. Familiarize yourself with the CAN-SPAM Act[7] and work to remain compliant.

VIDEO, 3D, AND VIRTUAL REALITY

I could just drone on and on about the importance of video, 3D tours, and virtual reality. It is clear from home buyer and consumer surveys that video is incredibly important for all industries because of how people shop today. The 2017 ViaSearch survey[8] of new home shoppers revealed that buyers want to see informational videos, virtual reality, and 3D tours. Seventy five to 80 percent of those surveyed indicated that these interactive visuals are very important to extremely important in the home shopping process.

Video has evolved a lot as more and more user-generated content is produced. Just think about how much video is recorded daily on Facebook Live. While it is important to have professional quality video on your website and social media to promote your brand and maintain your image. It is also important to have a mix of user-generated content that is more casual and more personal for social media sites.

Here are some other interesting stats from Hubspot[9]

- Four times as many customers would rather watch a video about a product than read about it.

- Almost 50 percent of internet users look for videos related to a product or service before visiting a store.

- Fifty-three percent of smartphone users feel more favorable towards companies whose mobile sites or apps provide instructional video content.

- Four out of five consumers believe that demo videos are helpful.

- Shoppers who view video are 1.81 times more likely to purchase than non-viewers.

Homebuilders, remodelers and others in the industry have lots of opportunity to utilize videos in their marketing. Here are some ideas:

- **Community videos.** Prospects love touring new home communities before they even step foot onsite. These videos can showcase the entrance, streetscape, amenities and give an overview of the lifestyle. Drones are used a lot to demonstrate the overall site plan and flow of the community from amenities to clubhouse to green space. Community videos are especially helpful for large master planned communities so that buyers get a feel for how it all ties together.

- **Model home video tours.** Get your agent to demonstrate the model on video or use voice over talent to describe the lifestyle and flow of the home. Show your prospects how living in one of your well thought out floor plans will make their hectic life easier. Shoot the front elevation and either lead them in through the front door, or give them a realistic view of what it is like to enter through the mud room from the garage and drop their stuff off in its specified area.

- **Pre-sale video.** So, the community isn't built yet, but you want to build a VIP list of leads and generate interest in your coming soon community. This video will help to tell the story of what is coming by showing area attractions (restaurants, shopping, etc.) as well as home plans and a site plan. Go ahead and tell the story to create excitement as you build toward a VIP event or grand opening.

- **Customer testimonials.** Get your happy customers to tell their story to prospective customers. Telling it on video increases validity while it makes it super easy to share to various sites and maximize exposure. Even better if you can shoot the video at their home. Anywhere works—front porch, living room, kitchen or back deck. Ask them to pick their favorite place in the home and then get them to talk about why it is their favorite place.

- **Product demonstration.** Show how your homes are built or demonstrate a specific product that is included in all of your homes. The sky is the limit here from pest control that is integrated into the walls of the house to green products or even a trendy new paint color.

- **3D and 360 model home tours.** Producing these tours requires a special camera that has the ability to rotate 360 degrees. Every room in the house is shot and from there a 3D dollhouse tour of the home is created that buyers can literally walk through a click at a time and see the entire home.

- **Virtual tours.** Show buyers a fully-furnished home without having to build it. Buyers can literally be in one model home looking at a different model with Google glasses or another virtual reality device! Buyers experience a realistic tour of your home, as if they were touring the actual model.

Make sure to promote all of your videos. Cross promoting on Pinterest, Facebook, YouTube, Twitter, etc. will garner additional views. Community and model home videos can be hot spot on interactive site plans. And, don't forget to include videos in all the appropriate places on your websites, as well as eblasts. Upload your videos to YouTube and use the embed code to put them other places. However, you will want to upload them directly some places, like Facebook.

What is the best length for a video? Most viewers prefer shorter videos, so the shorter you can make it the better. If you can say what you need to say and show all the appropriate visuals in 30 seconds, then you don't need to produce a two minute video.

Videohosting company Wistia[10] reports the following from their research:

- Two minutes is the sweet spot for videos. Engagement drops significantly after that. However, viewer engagement is steady up to the two minute mark. This means a viewer will give as much attention to a 90 second video as a 30 second video.

- For videos longer than two minutes, every second counts. Wistia research show significant drop off of views between two and three minutes. Keep your audience engaged by keeping it short.

- There is a second sweet spot for video views between six and 12 minutes. Of course, this most likely has to do with the content. For instance, these may be more in-depth videos that are targeted to specific audiences. Very long videos can be divided up into a series of shorter videos if the content allows.

Keep video viewers' attention longer by starting off energized and focusing on the important stuff. Don't wait until the end to give your Call to Action. You actually may want to include it in more than one place, including as a visual on the video screen.

MANAGING YOUR SOCIAL MEDIA PROGRAM 16

Who is going to manage your social media program? For companies with a fully-staffed marketing department, this might be an easy answer. Yet, even for companies with a marketing department, creating the volume of content needed for a successful social media program can be a challenge. Consider which option works better for your company: managing it in house or working with an agency. Both can work. It just depends on your needs.

MANAGING IN-HOUSE

More often than not, it will take a team to manage the social media program. It might consist of the marketing director, marketing assistant, online sales counselor and a sales agent or two. The size of your company and the duties and responsibilities of your team, as well as their talents and expertise will help to determine who on your team is best suited to do the day-to-day work.

Regardless of who manages the hands-on day-to-day tactics, you need one person to direct the strategy and keep the marketing plan on track. This is most likely going to be your marketing director. They should work with the content team to produce a content calendar that ties in with and complements the company's marketing plans.

Time commitment

Handling social media internally can be a huge time commitment, but it really depends on how many sites are being utilized and what the program entails. Budgeting 10–20 hours for someone who is a strong writer and already fairly familiar with all of the social media sites is a good starting point. The bulk of their time will be spent writing blogs and creating the monthly content calendar. The calendar will include every post that will go on every site, along with the link and the image that will be used. Having a calendar makes it easy to look at social media as part of the marketing big picture and time things to happen in unison.

Tools to help

Fortunately there are a lot of cool tools that can help make the creation and management of social media content easier. Here are some of our favorites along with a brief description of how we use them:

- **Canva.** Create stunning graphics to use on social media and other places. A myriad of templates for page headers, banners, flyers, etc. are available for use.

- **Facebook Pages App.** Perfect for managing your Facebook page when not in the office!

- **Hootsuite.** A platform for managing social media. The site currently supports social network integrations for Twitter, Facebook, Instagram, LinkedIn, Google+, YouTube, and others.

- **Latergram.** This is the closest thing to scheduling Instagram. You load the post, and it sets a reminder for you to live post it. You copy it from the app, and it automatically opens Instagram for you to post. This keeps you from having to email photos to yourself in order to post.

- **Picmonkey.** Photo editing and graphic design software that can be used to create collages and add text to images.

- **SocialJukebox.** An automated social media tool that we use to schedule evergreen tweets.

- **Sprout Social.** Social media management software that we use to schedule social media posts, respond to customers, track engagement and develop reports.

- **TweetDeck.** Allows you to sign in to multiple Twitter accounts and view their streams simultaneously. We use it to manage multiple Twitter accounts, schedule tweets and more.

WORKING WITH AN AGENCY

When does it make sense for a business to outsource its social media? Well, it really just depends. If your company is really small, it might make sense to outsource it instead of hiring another employee. If you have a small marketing department that is already over tasked it could be the perfect extension of that team.

There are a lot of benefits to hiring an agency:

- **Costs.** The cost associated with hiring a full time employee is (according to Glassdoor[1]) about three times more than the cost of hiring an agency to manage your social media. You could use interns or entry level employees to manage your social media, but there will be a lot of hands on training and a big time commitment on your part.

- **Meeting goals.** Your agency contact will be adept and writing content and managing social media because this is their expertise. They already know the nuances of each site because they use them multiple times a day for multiple clients. This means that they can achieve your goals faster than one person working for just one company.

- **Time.** Does anyone on your team have time to take on this task? Or should they be spending their time on tasks they already have?

- **Industry expertise.** Does the agency know your industry, or are they going to have to learn all of the lingo? Using an agency with experience in the industry you work will definitely streamline the process.

Remember that having a great social media presence doesn't just happen. It requires thought, strategy, and time. If your goals aren't being met because of time or lack of expertise, then outsource to a knowledgeable agency. If you are putting in effort, you need to be getting results. If you're not, hand it over to a firm that understands it. They can keep your social sites up-to-date and track engagement.

Before hiring an outside agency, do your research. Different agencies have different capabilities and different niches. Here are nine critical questions to consider in evaluating the competency of a social media marketing consultant or agency.

1 · Do they have a blog or news section on their website? Most seasoned social media marketers who can prove ROI understand how to build your program with the blog as the syndication engine. They should be actively using their blog as well. If their last blog post was in 2012, keep looking.

2 · When you Google the agency or consultant's name, what do you find? You should find results for both the company and the person. Don't trust your online reputation to a company that has not created a positive reputation of its own.

3 · What social media channels does the company or consultant use? They should be active on some combination of the following: Facebook, Twitter, LinkedIn, Pinterest, Instagram, YouTube, Google+, etc.

4 · What is the suggested strategy for using social media to achieve your overall marketing objectives? A competent social media marketer can build a strategy that works for your team. Social media marketing is not one size fits all. Your goals will probably vary greatly from your closest competitors. Your strategy should be part of an overall marketing plan.

5 · What kind of content do they write? Are they writing and posting content to the blog and social media sites that is unique to the clients they are writing for? Or is the content what I call features fluff that could go on any site within that industry?

6 · What training will the company or consultant offer to you and your team? They should be able to train your team to use various sites and tools with training materials they have developed. They should be able to answer your questions or know where to find the answers.

7 · Does the company or consultant understand SEO? Social media success is measured by traffic to your blog and website, and your ability to capture leads. They should have a basic understanding of how SEO works.

8 · Can the company show you examples of how it interconnects it strategy for clients? The ability to interconnect all of your sites increases their effectiveness exponentially. Ask for examples of client promotions that span multiple social sites, the client's website and advertising outlets.

9 · How do they show or prove ROI? Will they provide reports, or at least advice on what to measure? How will they know what is working and what isn't?

EVALUATING YOUR PROGRAM: TRACKING AND MEASURING RESULTS

Knowing what you want to achieve is the first step in achieving it. Setting goals allows you to create and maintain your social media program with intent. It is much easier to measure success if you set goals in the beginning. Knowing what information is available and how you are going to measure it is key in the process of setting up your social media and your overall marketing.

Ideally, the messages your company distributes through social media outlets are reaching target audiences and will produce measurable results. How you measure your social media campaign's success depends on your goals. Following are suggestions for measuring the ROI of the six goals for a social media marketing strategy we discussed in Chapter 3: Goal Setting:

1 · Increased website traffic

2 · Improved website search engine optimization

3 · Reputation management

4 · Engage with followers (customers, advocates, potential customers)

5 · Increased brand awareness

6 · Completed website contact forms

TRACK USERS

Once you have set your goals, you need to track the results. To gauge whether your website is meeting expectations for unique visitors, how much time they spend on the site, and the number of pages they visit, you need tracking software. Most websites and blogging platforms offer at least a rudimentary tool for this. For most websites, including a self-hosted WordPress blog, you can track performance with Google Analytics[1].

Review tracking data monthly, noting month-over-month and year-over-year trends. Besides measuring your blog's success; you will be able to see cyclical patterns in your online traffic. It may increase or decrease seasonally depending on your business. Pay attention to the following data:

- **Number of unique visitors.** What is the proportion of returning visitors to new visitors?

- **Average time on your site.** This can vary greatly depending on what they are looking for.

- **Number of pages (posts) each visitor views.** Note which types of content they spend the most time on and write more of it!

- **Referring sites.** These are the sites your visitors are coming from. Facebook, Twitter, and other websites where you promote your website should be sending you visitors. Google now records social traffic separately from referring sites.

- **Most popular content.** You can gauge readers' interests by the pages they land on, where they spend most of their time, and the pages from which they exit your site.

- **Visitors.** Use the map overlay feature to display the geographic region your traffic is coming from. You may learn surprising things about your visitors!

GOAL 1. INCREASED WEBSITE TRAFFIC

Using Google Analytics or another website tracking program, look at the traffic to your website. Track visitors from the social media sites and see their traffic patterns within your website. This data helps you identify which social media sites are sending the best quality traffic to your website. You should review it monthly and look at it month over month as well as year over year. An effective program will show slow, steady growth with some seasonal variation and sensitivity to economic conditions.

Visitors that click to your site from social media are typically more qualified, quality traffic. This is because they have already researched you online and you have typically made it into the consideration process if they have gotten to your website.

Measuring Website Traffic

1 · Number of unique visitors from social media—is it increasing?

2 · Share of overall traffic—how much of your overall traffic comes from social media?

3 · How much time do visitors spend on your site?

4 · What is the bounce rate of visitors from social media

5 · How many pages are your visitors viewing?

6 · What is the number of referring social media URLs?

7 · How many visitors click through to the "Contact Us" section?

8 · Is there an increase in traffic from the search engines?

GOAL 2. IMPROVED WEBSITE SEARCH ENGINE OPTIMIZATION

The relationship between SEO and social media often causes heated discussion. There is much debate on whether social media has a direct effect on search engine optimization. That said, we know without a doubt that Google uses links as one of its top ranking factors. Whether you post on Facebook, Twitter, or Pinterest, if you have high-quality content on social media sites, it is more likely to be linked to from other websites. And when people share links to your content, it helps your rankings. Having links back to your website from a variety of social media sites and blogs improves the site's credibility with the search engines and should increase traffic over time.

Since implementing the strategies discussed in this book, has the number of unique visitors to your site increased? A plan to post significant content online with links back to the company's main website probably was part of your strategy for reaching this goal. If the plan has been successful, your site visitors will come from a wider variety of searches and a larger number of social and referring URLs. You also may see more first-time site visitors than returning visitors.

Measuring Search Engine Optimization

1 · Has your website traffic increased?

2 · Has the number of inbound links to your website increased?

3 · Are there more referring sites now than there were before?

4 · Branded searches—are more people finding you by searching the name of your company?

GOAL 3. REPUTATION MANAGEMENT

It is important to have a strong reputation management program that proactively asks happy homeowners, agents, and partners to write reviews and provide testimonials. Do these reviews show up on Facebook, Yelp, Google+, and other sites? Have you been able to increase the number of positive reviews?

Another facet to reputation management is what happens when you Google your name. Are your page one SERP results all positive? If not, run a reputation management program to push negative results from SERPs below the first screen or even deeper into search results. Posting positive, relevant content on online sites that rank highly in the search engines is an effective way to mitigate the negative publicity. How long it takes to improve first-page results depends on the power of the negative results.

Measuring Reputation Management

1 · What is the number of reviews on Facebook (or other site) this year versus last?

2 · Has the percentage of positive reviews on Facebook increased over last year?

3 · Is there an increasing number of testimonial videos on your website?

4 · How many testimonials were added within the last year?

5 · What is the proportion of company-generated information in page one search results?

6 · Have negative search engine results moved to page two or lower of SERP?

GOAL 4. ENGAGE WITH FOLLOWERS

Social media should be social, right? How well are you doing engaging with your various groups of followers—customers, advocates, potential customers?

Specific target audiences will vary by company and even by the social media channel. Most of these tools keep tabs on the people subscribing to the user's content, whether they call them friends, followers, or fans. The quality of your followers is much more important than the quantity. Therefore, if you aren't following people who can buy from you or influence the buying decision of a potential customer, rethink your strategy.

Social media interactions improve brand perception as well as brand loyalty, so interact! If you want people to interact with you, not only do you need to respond and interact with them, but you need to write highly-engaging content.

Measuring Your Engagement with Followers

1 · Is the number of friends/followers/fans increasing?

2 · Do you have high-quality interactions? Are friends/followers/fans just receiving content, or are they actually engaged and participating?

3 · Are likes, shares, and comments per post increasing?

4 · Do you followers mention you? Are they sharing your content, or replying to your questions? And if so, do you reply to them?

Social media engagement can be tracked through the native social media platforms (Facebook Insights or Twitter analytics, for example) or you can use a social media management tool to help you. With tools like Sprout Social, Buffer, and Hootsuite, you can view each social media platform and see which posts were the most engaging.

Many social media monitoring companies provide monitoring and the ability to post to social sites from a consolidated dashboard. Their services and prices vary greatly, so research whether what they offer fits your needs and budget and whether it will help you reach your goals. Some monitoring companies charge a flat monthly fee; others price their services by how many individuals need simultaneous access to the dashboard and number of sites that are going to be connected.

You may want to consider the following social media monitoring companies:

- BuzzStream

- Cision

- Google Alerts

- Hootsuite

- Meltwater

- Radian 6

- Sprout Social

- Sysmos

- Thrive

- Trakur

GOAL 5. INCREASED BRAND AWARENESS

Social media is the perfect place to build brand awareness! Why? Well, the average person spends about two hours a day on social media sites[2]. You want to ensure that potential customers can find you online and that what they find represents your company. Social media helps marketers to have a better understanding of their brand's presence and reach. Most social media platforms now provide data on the reach of content, and this allows for more accurate reporting.

Measuring Brand Awareness

1 · How many people are following the brand?

2 · What is the reach of each post? What are my channels daily, weekly, monthly reach?

3 · Mentions, shares, and retweets—How many people are talking about your brand or sharing your social media posts?

4 · Positive representations of the company in many places online.

GOAL 6. COMPLETED WEBSITE CONTACT FORMS

If your social media program is successful in meeting goals 1–5, then you will probably achieve your ultimate goal: completed website contact forms, generating leads and sales. With customers researching more and more online before they buy, social media sites are playing a part in their research. Social media becomes part of your sales funnel. On your social sites, they can see how your treat existing buyers and prospects, as well as get the latest news. Getting these shoppers to fill out a contact form with their name, phone number, and email address turns them into a lead.

Measuring Completed Contact Forms

1 · How many leads (emails) have you collected through social media?

2 · Has the number of people who participate in your social media contest or events and shared their information with you increased?

3 · Is your website converting leads from social? Have you set up your Google Analytics to track completed website forms as a goal?

You should gain at least three other measurable ROIs from your online efforts:

1 · SERP. When you Google your name or other keyword phrases, you should see more of your results on page one.

2 · Enhanced brand. Your company will be recognized as readily online as in print.

3 · Increased efficiency. Your blog will serve as a syndication hub for content to social sites, your newsletter or eblasts, and your public relations. Instead of posting the same material three or four times on different sites, you can write one blog post and then post it with a slightly different introductory paragraph to each site.

WHAT'S NEXT? 18

Think about your email inbox. Now think about that person who constantly sends 400 or 500 word emails. Do you ever just want to respond tldr (too long; didn't read). You are not alone. The business leaders of tomorrow are already communicating differently. Attention spans have gotten shorter and shorter. However, our ability to consume information has sped up as we are continuously exposed to a growing stream of information. Of course both of these findings are even more evident in younger generations. The future will be fast[1]. Younger people scroll twice as fast as older generations. And people spend an average of 1.7 seconds looking at a piece of content. Most interestingly, people can recall content after only seeing it for .25 seconds.

The line between "internet user" and "social network user" will continue to blur. By 2020, seven out of 10 internet users will use social media. And the average age of this user will be 35[2].

Mobile is now and is the future as well. With 85 percent[3] of Americans already on mobile devices, the number of people browsing from handheld devices is going to continue to trend up. And up is good as long as your business has planned for it.

The appeal of mobile video will continue to grow especially as internet connections get faster and screens get better and the price comes down on both. A recent study shows that people will look at video on Facebook and Instagram five times longer than a static image. People are one and a half times more likely to watch video daily on a smartphone than on a computer[4].

Wearable technology will continue to advance. CCS Insight[5] has updated its future of wearable tech outlook, indicating that 411 million smart wearable devices, worth a staggering $34 billion, will be sold in 2020. These devices include eyewear, wristbands, tokens—clip ons and jewelry, wearable cameras, watches, and hearables."

Forget writing it down. Video and voice will be how we converse. Think back to early civilizations when people communicated by voice not in writing. By 2020, more than 75 percent of the world's mobile data traffic will be video. And through the power of voice, nearly one in three web browsing sessions is predicted to take place without a screen.

Video will continue to grow. To be successful, companies are going to need to produce videos and 3D tours. This is just a baby step toward what comes after that: virtual reality and augmented reality. Mobile video can quickly attract a buyer's attention. And as people's mobile viewing patterns evolve, consider planning around three types of experiences: "on the go" (short and snackable), "lean forward" interactive, and "lean back" (immersive).

User-generated content will continue to populate Facebook and Twitter streams. People like to share moments with their friends and family even when they are miles apart. Go Live options with Facebook, YouTube, and Instagram will continue to be popular as more and more people share content this way. One out of five videos on Facebook is generated through Facebook Live. And, the most popular YouTube videos are uploaded by individuals who prefer this live content style. In fact, nearly 80 percent of 18–34-year-olds and 71 percent of those 35 and older prefer live content[6]. Businesses will need to find ways to embrace their raving fans and get them to produce user-generated content that supports their marketing plans. Contests will get more creative.

Virtual reality is here. This is no longer a distant vision of the future. Builders are already using it. Interested buyers can visit the sales center to experience the virtual tour on a big screen TV. They simply wear virtual reality (VR) goggles and then they can see inside a home and walk around to experience it. Some builders have even set up kiosks at local malls to allow shoppers to take a break from shopping and tour their models. Internet users with Google Cardboard and other VR viewers can often tour VR models via the web from the comfort of their own home. People see VR becoming part of their everyday lives. In fact, more than 50 percent of the people surveyed think having VR means they will never miss anything important.

Visuals and images will continue to be important. Memes, GIFs, graphics, quotes and great photos are hugely popular. But there is a bigger picture we need to realize as marketers. People want to engage with content not just by their preferred method (Facebook, website, etc.) They want to consume the content the way they want it at that moment. For instance, I often "watch" videos at work on my local news channel. However, since I don't want to disturb the entire office, I usually choose to read the synopsis under the video. Another option would be to plug in my earbuds and just listen to the audio or even turn the sound off and simply read closed captions. You could call to make an appointment or text or instant message and achieve the same result. Embrace the senses and offer options of how to consume your content.

Social media advertising will skyrocket. If you are not yet advertising via social media, there is no time like the present. Advertising on these sites is cost effective for small and medium sized companies and this is a great way to amplify your marketing strategy. It is hard to move potential buyers off of the social sites and onto your website, so use social advertising to get them to convert.

Setting goals and creating a marketing plan now will set your company up for the future, and make it easier to incorporate new technology. The work you do now will pay off this year, and in years to come. As you look to the future, continue to find ways to embrace all of this digital media and incorporate it into your marketing plans.

NOTES

CHAPTER 1 | SOCIAL MEDIA IS EVERYWHERE

1. The Evolution of Technology (Pew Research Center, January 12, 2017) http://www.pewresearch.org/fact-tank/2017/01/12/evolution-of-technology/.

2. Shannon Greenwood, Andrew Perrin and Maeve Duggan, "Social Media Update 2016," Pew Research Center, November 11, 2016, http://www.pewinternet.org/2016/11/11/social-media-update-2016/.

3. "Social Media Fact Sheet," Pew Research Center, January 12, 2017, http://www.pewinternet.org/fact-sheet/social-media/.

4. "2017 ViaSearch New Home Buyer Report," ViaSearch, June 2017, accessed October 9, 2017, http://www.viasearch.com/.

CHAPTER 2 | THE BIG PICTURE

1. Masroor Ahmed, "Social Media Customer Service Statistics and Trends," *Social Media Today*, June 13, 2017, http://www.socialmediatoday.com/social-business/social-media-customer-service-statistics-and-trends-infographic.

CHAPTER 4 | REPUTATION MANAGEMENT

1. Khalid Saleh, "The Importance of Online Customer Reviews," Invesp, January 13, 2017, https://www.invespcro.com/blog/the-importance-of-online-customer-reviews-infographic/.

2. "Local Consumer Review Survey 2016", BrightLocal, accessed October 18, 2017, https://www.brightlocal.com/learn/local-consumer-review-survey/.

3. Sean Casey, "2016 Nielsen Social Media Report," *Insights* (blog), January 17, 2017, http://www.nielsen.com/us/en/insights/reports/2017/2016-nielsen-social-media-report.html.

CHAPTER 5 | MOBILE, VISUALS, AND HASHTAGS: SOCIAL MEDIA MUST-HAVES

1. "Mobile Fact Sheet," Pew Research Center, January 12, 2017, http://www.pewinternet.org/fact-sheet/mobile/.

2. Dillon Baker, "The 6 Most Important Social Media Trends of 2017," Contently, April 19, 2017, https://contently.com/strategist/2017/04/19/social-media-trends-2017/.

3. "YouTube for Press," YouTube, accessed October 19, 2017, https://www.youtube.com/intl/en-GB/yt/about/press/.

4. Dillon Baker, "The 6 Most Important Social Media Trends of 2017," Contently, April 19, 2017, https://contently.com/strategist/2017/04/19/social-media-trends-2017/.

5. Avi Salzman, "Snapchat Wants You to Call It a Camera Company," *Barron's Next*, February 17, 2017, http://www.barrons.com/articles/snapchat-wants-you-to-call-it-a-camera-company-1487371175.

6. Megan O'Neill, "The 2015 Video Marketing Cheat Sheet," *Animoto* (blog), May 7, 2015, https://animoto.com/blog/business/video-marketing-cheat-sheet-infographic/.

7. "Why Images Are So Important To Social Media," Medium, accessed October 19, 2017, https://medium.com/@onlinelogomaker/why-images-are-so-important-to-social-media-b9411dd678a8.

8. "Attention Span," Wikimedia Foundation, last edited October 5, 2017, 22:10, https://en.wikipedia.org/wiki/Attention_span.

CHAPTER 6 | FACEBOOK

1. Salman Aslam, "Facebook by the Numbers: Stats, Demographics & Fun Facts," Omnicore, August 11, 2017, https://www.omnicoreagency.com/facebook-statistics/.

2. Aslam, "Facebook by the Numbers."

3. Aslam, "Facebook by the Numbers."

4. Aslam, "Facebook by the Numbers."

5. Aslam, "Facebook by the Numbers,"

6. Aslam, "Facebook by the Numbers."

7. Aslam, "Facebook by the Numbers."

8. Aslam, "Facebook by the Numbers."

9. Aslam, "Facebook by the Numbers."

10. Aslam, "Facebook by the Numbers."

11. Josh Constine, "Facebook now has 2 billion monthly users. . . and responsibility," TechCrunch, June 27, 2017, https://techcrunch.com/2017/06/27/facebook-2-billion-users/.

12. Mandy Edwards, "20 Facebook Statistics for 2017," Business 2 Community, July 7, 2017, http://www.business2community.com/facebook/20-facebook-statistics-2017-01874493#orY6otxdxyWuEbgP.97.

13. "Distribution of Facebook users in the United States as of January 2017, by age group and gender," Statista, accessed Octber 19, 2017, https://www.statista.com/statistics/187041/us-user-age-distribution-on-facebook/.

14. Alex York, "7-Step Facebook Marketing Strategy to Dominate 2017," *Sprout Blog*, Sprout Social, April 10, 2017, https://sproutsocial.com/insights/facebook-marketing-strategy/.

CHAPTER 7 | TWITTER

1. Kurt Wagner, "Twitter added zero users last quarter," recode, July 27, 2017, https://www.recode.net/2017/7/27/16049084/twitter-jack-dorsey-q2-earnings-2017.

2. "Top 10 Twitter Statistics – September 2017," Zephoria, accessed October 19, 2017, https://zephoria.com/twitter-statistics-top-ten/.

3. "Customer Insights 2016: The value of a follower," Twitter + Research Now Whitepaper, accessed October 19, 2017, https://cdn.cms-twdigitalassets.com/content/dam/business-twitter/resources/Customer_insights_2016.pdf.

4. Salman Aslam, "Twitter by the Numbers: Stats, Demographics & Fun Facts," Omnicore, August 12, 2017, https://www.omnicoreagency.com/twitter-statistics/.

5. "What to Tweet," Twitter Business, accessed October 19, 2017, https://business.twitter.com/en/basics/what-to-tweet.html.

6. "Top 10 Twitter Statistics – September 2017," Zephoria, accessed October 19, 2017, https://zephoria.com/twitter-statistics-top-ten/.

7. "How Much Does it Cost to Advertise on Twitter," ThriveHive, February 21, 2017, https://thrivehive.com/how-much-does-it-cost-to-advertise-on-twitter/.

CHAPTER 8 | GOOGLE+ AND GOOGLE MY BUSINESS

1. "Google+," Wikimedia Foundation, last edited October 17, 2017, 15:04, https://en.wikipedia.org/wiki/Google%2B.

2. Robert Allen, "Search Engine Statistics 2017," *Smart Insights* (blog), April 13, 2017, http://www.smartinsights.com/search-engine-marketing/search-engine-statistics/.

3. "Google Plus Demographics & Statistics," Statistic Brain Research Institute, accessed October 19, 2017, http://www.statisticbrain.com/google-plus-demographics-statistics/.

CHAPTER 9 | LINKEDIN

1. Aatif Awan, "The Power of LinkedIn's 500 Million Member Community," *LinkedIn Official Blog,* LinkedIn, April 24, 2017, https://blog.linkedin.com/2017/april/24/the-power-of-linkedins-500-million-community.

2. Barb Darrow, "LinkedIn Claims Half a Billion Users," *Fortune,* April 24, 2017, http://fortune.com/2017/04/24/linkedin-users/.

3. "The Ultimate List of Marketing Statistics," HubSpot, accessed October 19, 2017, https://www.hubspot.com/marketing-statistics.

4. "Social Media Fact Sheet," Pew Research Center, January 12, 2017, http://www.pewinternet.org/fact-sheet/social-media/.

5. "Social Media Fact Sheet," January 12, 2017.

6. Salman Aslam, "LinkedIn by the Numbers: Stats, Demographics & Fun Facts," Omnicore, January 24, 2017, https://www.omnicoreagency.com/linkedin-statistics/.

CHAPTER 10 | PINTEREST

1. Shannon Greenwood, Andrew Perrin and Maeve Duggan, "Social Media Update 2016," Pew Research Center, November 11, 2016, http://www.pewinternet.org/2016/11/11/social-media-update-2016/.

2. Greenwood, Perrin, and Duggan, "Social Media Update 2016."

3. "10 reasons why your business needs to be on Pinterest," *Pinterest Business* (blog), September 16, 2015, https://business.pinterest.com/en/blog/10-reasons-why-your-business-needs-to-be-on-pinterest.

4. "New measurement solutions show how intent turns to action on Pinterest," *Pinterest Business* (blog), June 14, 2017, https://business.pinterest.com/en/blog/new-measurement-solutions-show-how-intent-turns-to-action-on-pinterest.

5. Rachel Eisenberg, "Pinterest and the Power of Future Intent," Kantar Millward Brown, May 12, 2015, https://www.millwardbrowndigital.com/pinterest-and-the-power-of-future-intent/.

6. "10 reasons why," September 16, 2015.

7. Salman Aslam, "Pinterest by the Numbers: Stats, Demographics & Fun Facts," Omnicore, January 23, 2017, https://www.omnicoreagency.com/pinterest-statistics/.

8. "Christmas in July: It's time to try search ads on Pinterest," *Pinterest Business* (blog), July 31, 2017, https://business.pinterest.com/en/blog/christmas-in-july-its-time-to-try-search-ads-on-pinterest.

9. "10 reasons why," September 16, 2015.

10. "New measurement solutions," June 14, 2015.

11. "150 million people finding ideas on Pinterest," *Pinterest* (blog), October 13, 2016, https://blog.pinterest.com/en/150-million-people-finding-ideas-pinterest.

12. Aslam, "Pinterest by the Numbers."

13. Aslam, "Pinterest by the Numbers."

14. Greenwood, Perrin, and Duggan, "Social Media Update 2016."

15. Aslam, "Pinterest by the Numbers."

16. Aslam, "Pinterest by the Numbers."

17. "New measurement solutions," June 14, 2015.

18. "Christmas in July," July 31, 2017.

19. "10 reasons why," September 16, 2015.

20. "Why Pinterest ads work," *Pinterest Business*, accessed October 22, 2017, https://business.pinterest.com/en/why-pinterest-ads-work.

CHAPTER 11 | HOUZZ

1. Craig Smith, "17 Impressive Houzz Statistics and Facts," DMR, July 5, 2017, https://expandedramblings.com/index.php/houzz-statistics/#.WePaCzu1thE.

2. "Advertise on Houzz," Houzz, accessed October 19, 2017, https://www.houzz.com/advertiseOnHouzz.

3. "Advertise on Houzz," October 19, 2107.

4. "Houzz Launches Trade Program," Houzz, June 6, 2017, https://www.houzz.com/press/332/Houzz-Launches-Trade-Program.

5. "Welcome to Houzz," Houzz, accessed October 19, 2017, https://www.houzz.com/aboutUs.

6. "Build Your Business with Houzz," Houzz, accessed October 19, 2017, https://www.houzz.com/pro.

7. Smith, "17 Impressive Houzz Statistics."

8. Smith, "17 Impressive Houzz Statistics,"

9. Lori Aitkenhead, "8 Ways Home Builders Can Use Houzz for Lead Generation," *Marketing Blog*, HubSpot, updated October 19, 2017, https://blog.hubspot.com/marketing/houzz-for-lead-generation.

10. "Houzz Launches Trade Program," June 6, 2017.

CHAPTER 12 | INSTAGRAM

1. Karissa Bell, "Instagram just blew through another important milestone," Mashable, September 25, 2017, http://mashable.com/2017/09/25/instagram-800-million/?#.eSJdeMSIOqo.

2. "Social Media Fact Sheet," Pew Research Center, January 12, 2017, http://www.pewinternet.org/fact-sheet/social-media/.

3. "Announcing 15 Million Business Profiles," *Business Blog*, Instagram Business, July 26, 2017, https://business.instagram.com/blog/announcing-15-million-business-profiles.

4. "Announcing 15 Million Business Profiles," July 26, 2017.

5. "Announcing 15 Million Business Profiles," July 26, 2017.

6. "Unfiltered: Looking at Instagrammers through a Biometric Lens," Facebook IQ, April 12, 2017, https://www.facebook.com/iq/articles/unfiltered-looking-at-instagrammers-through-a-biometric-lens?ref=wpinsights_rd.

7. Salman Aslam, "Instagram by the Numbers: Stats, Demographics & Fun Facts," Omnicore, August 10, 2017, https://www.omnicoreagency.com/instagram-statistics/.

8. "Celebrating One Year of Instagram Stories," (Instagram Press (blog), Instagram, August 2, 2017, https://instagram-press.com/blog/2017/08/02/celebrating-one-year-of-instagram-stories/.

9. Emily Weisberg, "How to Post Videos to Instagram," ThriveHive, June 15, 2017, https://thrivehive.com/how-to-post-videos-to-instagram/.

10. "Hashtags for #homebuilder in Instagram, Twitter, Facebook, Tumblr, ello," Top-Hashtags.com, accessed October 19, 2017, https://top-hashtags.com/hashtag/homebuilder/.

CHAPTER 13 | SNAPCHAT

1. Artyom Dogtiev, "Snapchat Revenue and Usage Statistics 2017," Business of Apps, updated August 29, 2017, http://www.businessofapps.com/data/snapchat-statistics/.

2. Biz Carson, "Here's everything you need to know about how many people are using Snapchat," Business Insider, February 2, 2017, http://www.businessinsider.com/how-many-people-use-snapchat-user-numbers-2017-2.

3. Salman Aslam, "Snapchat by the Numbers: Stats, Demographics & Fun Facts," Omnicore, August 12, 2017, https://www.omnicoreagency.com/snapchat-statistics/.

4. Aslam, "Snapchat by the Numbers."

5. Aslam, "Snapchat by the Numbers."

6. Aslam, "Snapchat by the Numbers."

7. Aslam, "Snapchat by the Numbers."

CHAPTER 14 | YOUTUBE

1. "YouTube Company Statistics," Statistic Brain Research Institute, accessed October 19, 2017, http://www.statisticbrain.com/youtube-statistics/.

2. YouTube Company Statistics," accessed October 19, 2017.

3. "9 Best YouTube User Statistics for Marketers," *The YouTube and Influencer Marketing Blog*, mediakix, accessed October 19, 2017, http://mediakix.com/2017/03/youtube-user-statistics-demographics-for-marketers/#gs.=nUhe10.

4. "YouTube Company Statistics," accessed October 19, 2017.

5. "YouTube Company Statistics," accessed October 19, 2017.

6. "YouTube Company Statistics," accessed October 19, 2017.

7. Celie O'Neil-Hart and Howard Blumenstein, "The Latest Video Trends: Where Your Audience is Watching," think with Google, April 2016, https://www.thinkwithgoogle.com/consumer-insights/video-trends-where-audience-watching/.

8. "9 Best YouTube User Statistics," accessed October 19, 2017.

9. "9 Best YouTube User Statistics," accessed October 19, 2017.

10. O'Neil-Hart and Blumenstein, "The Latest Video Trends."

11. "9 Best YouTube User Statistics," accessed October 19, 2017.

12. "9 Best YouTube User Statistics," accessed October 19, 2017.

13. "9 Best YouTube User Statistics," accessed October 19, 2017.

CHAPTER 15 | OTHER DIGITAL MARKETING

1. "The Podcast Consumer 2017," Edison Research and Triton Digital, accessed October 19, 2017, http://www.edisonresearch.com/wp-content/uploads/2017/04/Podcast-Consumer-2017.pdf.

2. "The Ultimate List of Marketing Statistics," Hubspot, accessed October 19, 2017, https://www.hubspot.com/marketing-statistics.

3. Matt Secrist, "5 Ways a Blog Can Help Your Business Right Now," Search Engine Journal, May 13, 2017, https://www.searchenginejournal.com/benefits-of-blogging-for-business/195037/.

4. "Email Marketing Benchmarks," MailChimp, accessed October 19, 2017, https://mailchimp.com/resources/research/email-marketing-benchmarks/.

5. "Marketing e-mail open and click rates in the United States in 2016, by degree of personalization," Statista, accessed October 19, 2017, https://www.statista.com/statistics/260678/e-mail-open-click-rates-personalization/.

6. Daniel Burstein, "Email Research Chart: How often customers want to receive promotional emails," MarketingSherpa, February 10, 2015, https://www.marketingsherpa.com/article/chart/how-customers-want-promo-emails.

7. "CAN-SPAM Act: A Compliance Guide for Business," Federal Trade Commission, accessed October 23, 2017, https://www.ftc.gov/tips-advice/business-center/guidance/can-spam-act-compliance-guide-business.

8. "2017 ViaSearch New Home Buyer Report," ViaSearch, June 2017, http://www.viasearch.com/.

9. "The Ultimate List of Marketing Statistics," Hubspot, accessed October 19, 2017, https://www.hubspot.com/marketing-statistics.

10. Ezra Fishman, "How Long Should Your Next Video Be?" *Wistia Blog*, Wistia, July 5, 2016, https://wistia.com/blog/optimal-video-length.

CHAPTER 16 | MANAGING YOUR SOCIAL MEDIA PROGRAM

1. "Social Media Manager Salaries," Glassdoor, updated October 16, 2017, https://www.glassdoor.com/Salaries/social-media-manager-salary-SRCH_KO0,20.htm.

CHAPTER 17 | EVALUATING YOUR PROGRAM: TRACKING AND MEASURING RESULTS

1. "Get started with Analytics," Google Analytics Help, accessed October 23, 2017, https://support.google.com/analytics/answer/1008015?hl=en.

2. Laura Forer, "How Much Time Do People Spend on Social Media," MarketingProfs, April 14, 2017, https://www.marketingprofs.com/chirp/2017/31864/how-much-time-do-people-spend-on-social-media-infographic.

CHAPTER 18 | WHAT'S NEXT?

1. "Shifts for 2020: Multisensory Multipliers," Facebook IQ, June 22, 2017, https://www.facebook.com/iq/articles/shifts-for-2020-multisensory-multipliers.

2. Dillon Baker, "The 6 Most Important Social Media Trends of 2017," Contently, April 19, 2017, https://contently.com/strategist/2017/04/19/social-media-trends-2017/.

3. Shan Wang, "85 percent of Americans us mobile devices to access news – and seniors are driving that number up," NiemanLab, June 12, 2017, http://www.niemanlab.org/2017/06/85-percent-of-americans-use-mobile-devices-to-access-news-and-seniors-are-driving-that-number-up/.

4. "Moving Pictures: The Persuasive Power of Video," Facebook IQ, March 8, 2017, https://www.facebook.com/iq/articles/moving-pictures-the-persuasive-power-of-video.

5. Paul Lamkin, "Wearable Tech Market to be Worth $34 Billion by 2020," Forbes, February 17, 2016, https://www.forbes.com/sites/paullamkin/2016/02/17/wearable-tech-market-to-be-worth-34-billion-by-2020/#5e2dfd6d3cb5.

6. Gillian Heltai, "What Millenials' YouTube Usage Tells Us about the Future of Video Viewership," comScore, June 23, 2016, https://www.comscore.com/Insights/Blog/What-Millennials-YouTube-Usage-Tells-Us-about-the-Future-of-Video-Viewership.

INDEX

4Ps, 7, 10
3D, 5, 8, 9, 31, 91, 96, 105, 107, 124

A

Adobe Spark, 34
advertising, 8, 9, 12, 17–18, 19, 21, 40, 43, 46, 59–60,
  68, 73, 80, 84, 85–86, 92, 113, 125
 agency, 11, 109, 111–113
 pay-per-click, 8, 18, 60
 paid, 17–18, 19, 59–60, 68, 73, 80, 85–86,
   92
analytics, 72, 73, 76, 99, 116, 120, 121
Angie's List, 5, 6, 25
Askimet, 98
Audacity, 97
Avid Ratings, 27

B

BeFunky, 34
Best of the Web, 101
blog, 9, 10, 11–12, 16, 19, 21, 23, 26, 37, 38, 40, 41,
  50, 53, 57, 59, 60, 65, 67, 69, 72, 73, 89, 91, 92,
  96, 97–101, 110, 112, 116, 117, 122
 compounding post, 97
 content for, 10–11, 97, 98, 99, 100
 keywords, 98, 99
 post, 12, 16, 57, 59, 66, 96, 100–101, 103,
   122
 promote, 12, 40, 50, 67, 72, 101
 plug-ins for, 98–99
 RSS, 101
 schedule for, 11–12, 97–98
 sharing, 101
 syndicate, 57, 98, 122
Blog Catalog, 101
brand, 7, 9, 10, 12, 19, 20–21, 38, 40, 47, 52, 53, 58,
  59, 63, 64, 65, 66, 67, 79, 80, 83–84, 85, 87, 92,
  103, 104, 105, 118, 120–121, 122
 advocate, 14, 20
 ambassadors, 20
 awareness, 16, 21, 80, 115, 120–121
 consistency, 47, 52, 53, 65, 92
Breadcrumb NavXT, 99
Buffer, 120
BuzzStream, 120

C

Call to Action (CTA), 9, 30, 33, 35, 39, 41, 60, 85, 92,
  101, 103, 104, 107
CAN-SPAM Act, 104–105
Canva, 33, 34, 110
campaigns, 9, 18, 21, 24, 38, 40, 45, 46, 68, 78, 80,
  102, 105, 115
 advertising, 9, 46, 68, 80
 marketing, 38, 102
 reputation management, 18, 24
 social media, 21, 45, 46, 68, 78, 80, 105,
   115
Cision, 120
complaints, customer, 5, 12, 13, 18, 28, 39
 responding to, 28, 39
Constant Contact, 104
contact us form, 8–9, 15, 16, 21, 117, 121–122